FINISHING STRONG

Strategies For Baby Boomers
To Transform Dreams Into Realities

Gwendolyn Cody-Davis

Love, Joy & Peace
G. Cody - Davis

NOMOLAC, LLC

Finishing Strong
Strategies For Baby Boomers To Transform Dreams Into
Realities
© 2023 by Gwendolyn Cody-Davis

Printed in the United States of America
ISBN: 978-1-7346793-3-5
Published by: NOMOLAC, LLC.
Copy Editor: Zelda Oliver-Miles
Developer Editor: Dr. Joel Boyce (@jcbedpro on Instagram)
Cover Photos: Kim Brundage Photography
Interior Formatting & Cover Design: Zelda Oliver-Miles

Dedication

To my African king, Randy Matthew Davis.

Thanks for your love and support for our family, but most of all, I am thankful that you are in love with the Lord.

ACKNOWLEDGMENTS

First and foremost, I thank God, my heavenly Father, who provides creativity and power to get wealth.

I thank my very best friend in the whole world. I call him my African king, Randy M. Davis. I am so delighted that the Lord made sure he found me.

I thank God for Bishop Charles E. Wiley and his lovely wife, Amelia, of Blessed Hope Community Church (BHCC) in Prince George, Virginia for their superior spiritual leadership. I am more than grateful for my BHCC family.

I thank and praise God for my loving mother, Thelma L. Cody, my siblings, Booker T. Hall and Tangela Cody, my sons, Ryan and Reagan, their beautiful wives, Kiandra and Jessica, and my entire family. The prayer of righteous people avails, and I have been sustained as a result.

I am sending a special shout out to my mentor and coach Jasmine Womack. Jasmine's priceless leadership and her enthusiasm to see God's people accomplish God's plan is extraordinary. Hats off to her anointed team of coaches as well.

Again, I thank God that I now realize that everything He states in His Word is everything I can accomplish if I keep Him first. I thank Him also because He is not a respecter of persons.

Contents

INTRODUCTION

"God began doing a good work in you, and I am sure he
will continue it until it is finished when Jesus Christ
comes again."
— *Philippians 1:6*

W hat would you do if you knew you would not
fail? Have you ever believed in yourself so
much that you knew your self-confidence and work ethic
would make your dreams come true?

I have not always been that person, but I am now. I
have found that if you are truly committed and focused
on your dream, your dream will become a reality. You've
probably heard someone say a thousand times, "It
doesn't matter how you start something; it's how you

finish it that matters." Between the birth date and the death date, you have the opportunity to show the world that your time on Earth was not a mistake. You are here to make a powerful impact and to make God even prouder. Leading others, believing in others, and teaching what you have learned and experienced on the way to the realization of your dreams are steps in the right direction.

Despite your best efforts to stay the course, distractions are designed strategically to keep you stuck in a state of no progress. It seems that they come at a time when you are ready to reposition yourself in your life. Perhaps you have made daily affirmations, glimpsed your next level, and posted them on social media. Even your vision board reflects the new and exciting goals that you have set. However, out of nowhere comes a situation large enough to divert your attention, energy, and even your faith from something you wholeheartedly desire to accomplish.

All distractions are not to be viewed negatively. Some distractions such as making yourself laugh can help you redirect your thoughts and make you feel lighter inside. However, some distractions can get you sidetracked, which means you must examine your position carefully and determine how you will navigate your path.

I have made a conscious decision to finish strong. It has become my mantra because I perceive this race is not for the faint of heart. I must be strong to finish well, and that does not happen overnight. My dedication speaks volumes about my life journey once I comprehended that if I make one consistent step after another, I will reach my goals. It is my hope and prayer that you will finish strong as well. Perseverance through adversity will enable you to pivot and move forward, so giving up is not an option.

You are exactly where you should be while you are waiting for your golden opportunity to soar. One of the most significant things to remember is that you are important, and it's time to show up and be ready to take control. Sitting on the sidelines and watching others play and win is one thing, but what about your dream? When will it be a win for you?

Though distractions will come, you should make a superior decision to dig deep within and visualize expanding your territory as you grow in wisdom. Get in the habit of looking forward to the possibilities and looking back only to show gratitude or provide testimonies to others because you will arrive at your destination not a minute late. Your limitations are governed only by what you allow to restrict you. The sky is not your limit if you are willing to go the distance and if your belief is in the limitless power of Father God.

It is important to know your value, and it is also important not to allow anyone to devalue you. Tiny dots become lines. Lines become surfaces, planes, and shapes. Your value is not based on your tiny dots. Your value is based on the seeds you sow along your journey and the surfaces, planes, and shapes. Elevate your faith to believe you can complete every good work you feel compelled to accomplish and inspire others to do the same.

You might not have a perfect life, but life changes the minute your mind changes. If you can visualize how you want your life to be, you can achieve it. Whatever you set your mind to do, you can do it. There is no need for your life to mirror anyone else's life — it just has to be distinctively your life.

Remember that finishing strong is an attitude. Do you believe you can? Are you courageous enough to cross the finish line? Will you be able to see moving forward despite setbacks and difficulties?

Believe that your life's journey is not a one-hit wonder. Your destiny hinges on greatness. Why? The world is counting on you and the flavor you bring that adds value to your space and those around you.

Ecclesiastes 7:8 lets us know "It is better to finish something than to start it. It is better to be patient than to be proud."

ONE

The Power Of Small Beginnings

"The people should not think that small beginnings are unimportant. They will be happy when they see Zerubbabel with tools, building the Temple."
— Zechariah 4:10a

Great things begin from small, almost insignificant beginnings. In the beginning, you were just a tiny dot. It was God's mind that determined you would be designed uniquely with purpose and passion. Even though you started as a seed, if anyone ever told you that you wouldn't blossom into a mighty harvest, I hope you know now that they were telling lies.

I was a small town girl with big ideas and big dreams. I was born and raised in Thomasville, Georgia, known as City of Roses, I am the middle child of four. The middle child has been said to be independent and possess negotiation skills and peacemaking abilities. I appreciate how the atmosphere of my hometown helped guide me to my present reality. Although I am from a small town, I did not have small faith.

Early on in my life, I developed a positive attitude and my faith began as a mustard seed. I was too young to realize that both were key ingredients of a great life. It just seemed natural to me to be positive. It was easy for me to place my faith in God because of the relationship I developed with Him. In addition to wanting my parents, family, and my entire village to be proud of me, I do admit I was sometimes overly concerned about pleasing people. I wanted everyone to like me.

It is with great pride that I say I was a church girl. In Sunday School, at the worship service, and at Baptist Training Union, I learned so many life lessons. What I didn't realize at the time was that I was being shaped, molded, and prepared for my future. When asked recently by a friend, "Did you think you would become an author, a speaker, and use other gifts you have yet to unwrap?" My response was, "Not really, but I knew I wanted to speak and travel the world; I loved meeting people, and I am fascinated by other cultures."

FUNDAMENTALS

My parents and my paternal grandmother made sure

I had a solid Christian foundation. They taught me how to love God, His Word, and others. My anchor is still that solid foundation to this day. My husband Randy and I taught our sons, Ryan and Reagan, the same core values of God, family, and community.

I love my hometown, but I knew I wanted to live in a big city because there were more opportunities to explore. As a child, I dreamed of visiting and living in places like New York, London, and Paris. Little did I know I would visit New York many times, and I would visit London and Paris too. When I was a junior in high school, I wasn't sure what I wanted to do after graduation. I loved keypunching, but I did not know it was a career option. One of my neighborhood friends, who was like a younger brother to me, accompanied me to the public library one day, and my interest was piqued by something that caught my eye in a career book.

Through the 1970s, keypunch operators, also known as data transcribers, still were used commonly for both data and program entry. After further research, I found that I could apply to Atlanta Technical School to receive the training that would equip me for such a position.

Though it was my starting point, I felt content that I had discovered my niche. I started making plans to move the day after graduation. Excitement filled my heart. I could hardly wait. Some of my friends were going to college, and most of them were staying in state; but a seed was planted in my mind to move to Atlanta (also in state); I had visited there for spring break during my early high school years.

It was super cool to have older siblings who were already out of the house and getting settled. I enjoyed being able to visit them over summer break. I spent two summers working with my oldest sister, Jewelry, in St. Petersburg, Florida. At the time, she worked for a large hotel chain as an executive housekeeper. I know I surprised her when my work ethic began to speak for me. I wasn't used to domestic work. It was a summer gig for me, but I enjoyed learning how to clean rooms, work in the laundry room, and do all the other things that went along with being a hotel housekeeper. I developed time management and basic maintenance skills as a summer hire in the housekeeping department. Since this position taught me how to interact positively with hotel guests, my customer service skills quickly developed.

The summer prior to my senior year of high school, I was blessed to get a summer job at the Veterans Administration, which was also in St. Petersburg, Florida. A close family friend who worked in human resources told me about the position and helped me complete my application and prepare for the interview. I was a proud summer hire. I began my career in the federal government as a clerk-typist.

RIGHT EXPOSURE

A book club that I was a member of when I was about ten years old helped me formulate big ideas mentally. Each month, a different book provided information from a different country, and I was all in. I wanted to experience different cultures, and I wondered what it would be like to visit abroad. I never imagined that I would become a military spouse and travel the world, meet new people, learn new languages, and experience new things. God saw my desire, and He granted it to me without me being aware of it.

I had no clue that my work as a data transcriber would allow me to develop excellent grammar skills and a strong attention to detail. I became an outstanding secretary for many years because of my keypunch operator experience. I never imagined I would be working for the federal government for thirty-plus years. I spent over twelve years with two agencies as a customer account specialist, resolving customer problems every day.

THE YOUNG MILITARY WIFE

Looking back on my humble beginnings as a wife, if I could speak to the twenty-year-old Gwen, I would say to her, "Do not compare yourself to anyone." It was a huge mistake, but I made it. There are days when I long to return to those humble beginnings. In spite of having friends our age — in their early twenties — we tended to gravitate towards older couples. In those days, older military couples were thirty-five to thirty-nine years old. Being around them helped us build a strong foundation for our relationship and marriage. To this very day, we thank God for a very special couple, who we now call our military parents, Ned and Eula Salter. They were the best examples on the planet, both abroad and stateside. They have and continue to encourage and add joy to our lives. However, the twenty-year-old Gwen was very materialistic, and she wanted what the senior military members had, not realizing they started out as young couples like we did and agreed to take consistent steps towards achieving their goals, raising their families, and having a wonderful life.

While living life backwards is not an option, there are times I wish I had the wisdom I have now. It is clear to me why wisdom is the principal thing. I also can attest that nothing beats experience. Start small and take tiny steps with a strategic plan in place to grow and develop. There is no shame in that. If you're starting a business, ministry, non-profit, book club, travel club, or whatever your heart desires, make sure you invite wisdom. Even if your first step is small, ensure that it is intentional, and more importantly, commit to the process fully.

TINY STEPS

I have a new saying, "There is absolutely nothing wrong with taking tiny steps, thinking bigger thoughts, and learning rapidly." Remember that your faith started small. If you regard faith as one of your greatest virtues, you will notice it is growing and developing. Mustard seeds measure one to two millimeters in diameter. However, the brush growth can reach heights and widths of twenty to thirty feet. There is nothing wrong with the mustard seed faith. Your faith goal should include witnessing a tiny mustard seed flourishing into a big beautiful bush. By using faith daily on your journey, you start believing in more faith, and before you know it, your faith expands and rises to every occasion. Starting from a tiny dot, everyone is capable of achieving success with the proper guidance and work ethic.

During my elementary, junior high, and high school years, I enjoyed celebrating at the end of the school year when I worked hard and tirelessly. I realized though that it would take more than one class and a study group session to achieve not only passing a class with a high grade, but also absorbing the material and being able to apply it in the real world.

A large mindset pays large dividends when you start small. It is said that greatness is always hidden in the small things, and big gifts sometimes come in small packages. Those who understand the seed principle or the way seeds reproduce after their kind will realize that the best impact can be made by the smallest seed sown in the right soil. Embrace the power of small beginnings and be flexible in the process.

It was my intention to create a coffee table book instead of the book you're reading. I shared the concept with a few people close to me. I could see it. I liked it, and I wanted to share it with the world. It would be full of poetry and in my eyes, big aha moments. I was looking for an illustrator and the whole nine yards. However, as I made a huge shift in my life and invested in a new coaching program, I realized even before being advised by my mentor that it was not the book for now.

The small step you feel directed to take sometimes comes from a small voice. I had to rewind, reset, and dig deep inside myself. I even did some breathing exercises because I had a strong will to work on that project (the coffee table book). When I prayed for my "now book," the Lord led me to the right place to receive the proper guidance to make yet another tiny step toward my destiny.

My foundation was one thing I wanted to get right from the start. Solid foundations cannot be overstated. If you are building, and your foundation is not reliable, trouble will be on the horizon. That is one of the things I love about starting small. It allows you to build what God has instructed you to build.

We all experience seasons in which we feel unmotivated. During a slump, you might feel stuck, which can cause negative emotions, but that's a good time to push through. Don't forget to celebrate every win.

No matter where you are on life's journey, from your first step to the pinnacle, there is always something to learn and teach. Your victories will keep you winning, and God will take you to new levels.

I am so grateful that those who come into contact with me today still experience the childlike attitude and faith I developed at an early age. While this journey called life is challenging at times, I encourage others to remain calm. I also have noticed how others are blessed when they see me continue to take tiny steps of faith.

TRUST AND BELIEVE

Are you embracing the power of small beginnings? Put your trust in God, decide never to doubt Him, and keep an attitude of gratitude. Trusting God means you've already surrendered your will and power to Him. Trusting in Father God does not mean doing nothing; rather, it means co-laboring with him. Why not collaborate? Seeing Him as your trust element, He leads and guides you on your journey from the first step to the next.

The Bible tells us in Job 8:7, "Where you began is unimportant, because your future will be so successful." As I hear these words, I am overjoyed because I realize the Divine destiny of God. I can put my doubts, anxieties, and fears to rest knowing what His word reveals about my future.

Gratitude keeps you grounded. It could be as simple as journaling the five top things you are thankful for daily and reflecting on them. Being in good health, physically and mentally, and having the opportunity to spend quality time with your loved ones probably will top the list. While working on your next step, being grateful for where you are even in your humble beginnings is key to your overall success.

T W O

Overcoming Failures

"Do not be embarrassed by your failures, learn from them and start again."
—Richard Branson

Have you ever felt that everyone around you was progressing except for you? Perhaps you felt defeated. Maybe your focus or goals were dim, or perhaps you could not accomplish what you set out to do. You are not alone if you have ever felt helpless and hopeless. Having walked in these shoes many times, I know how they feel.

In fifth grade, I started noticing some of my strengths and weaknesses academically. I have to admit that the school year was a bit traumatic for me. It wasn't until adulthood that I realized what really happened. I am aware of how you can block root causes or traumatic experiences from your mind until you feel they haven't occurred. The truth is, you know they did.

Academically, I had always been at the top of my game. I loved school in those days. As a first grader, I attended East Side Elementary. The following year, a new elementary school was built next to East Side. I was elated to be one of the first classes to attend Scott Elementary. I felt balanced in all of my subjects. During this period, I developed my self-confidence and excelled in all my classes. The ratio of Caucasians to African Americans was probably 9:1. Being in the one percent was not an issue for me or for my family. Parents could send their child to any school they chose. My parents sent me to school on our side of town. I was happy with that. Other parents sent their children to predominantly Black schools. It worked out in some cases since those were the closest schools to their homes.

LIFE IS FULL OF TRANSITIONS

During my fifth-grade year, we were undergoing integration, and now that I look back, maybe that experience threw me off track. I did not experience African American teachers until that school year.

My weakness in math was evidenced that school year, but my ten-year-old self thought it would go away. It didn't happen. For the first time I made a D on my report card. At this tender age, I had an internal war and didn't verbalize it, so I silently developed math anxiety and fear. I excelled in my other classes. I especially loved English and social studies, and I literally could memorize poems, long speeches, or anything else you put before me. Math was a concept I wasn't able to grasp.

Again, the adult Gwen knows that if your foundation is weak, your building will crumble. My sixth-grade year was so much better compared to my fifth-grade year. I had the best math teacher in the world, Ms. Donovan. The entire year, I maintained a B average, but junior high proved to be challenging for me.

There were no social media platforms at that time, but that didn't mean we didn't compete, emulate, or compare ourselves with each other. Among my friends, no one wanted to stand out so much that it attracted attention, especially the wrong kind of attention.

At the end of eighth-grade, we were planning our class schedules for our freshman year. All kinds of emotions were being expressed by my friends and me, including excitement, fear, and joy. The buzzwords for math for upcoming freshmen were either Algebra I or Geometry. My eighth-grade math year ended in a total failure for me. It felt like my building was crumbling one brick at a time.

I attended summer school for two summers just for math reinforcement. I do believe that helped. But, there was something I did that didn't help. I began to feel that I was not college material, and I questioned how far I would make it in the world without a strong ability to master mathematics.

As I think about it now, maybe a tutor would have helped me. Nonetheless, I recall feeling attacked by my self-confidence. On top of that, I was chubby. In spite of my mom's best efforts, she was limited in her ability to help me because she didn't understand the "new math" as it was identified.

LEARNING FROM MISTAKES

The worst mistake I made was listening to friends about the subjects they would take during our freshman year. When it was time to sign up for my ninth-grade classes, I ignored the fact that I didn't pass Introduction to Algebra. As a result, I had my logic, negative energy, and the enemy of my dream speaking at the same time to me.

What is so bazaar is that all of these voices were speaking to me and telling me that I was the only one who didn't get it. Did I listen? Yes. Did they help to slow me down at all? In all honesty, yes. The fear of math built up for the next three years, my freshman through my junior years. My foundation was not solid, and I felt lost in the shuffle.

Pride and embarrassment do not equal redemption, but God saw me. He knew me, and He created me to be more than what I was experiencing during those years. Until I realized I had to go back to the basics, I literally continued missing the mark. Even though the math classes I needed to take were not college-bound courses (as I had been taking all the ones that were), I needed to gain a basic understanding of basic mathematics. The only math skills I felt I had were addition, subtraction, multiplication, and division. In fact, I learned my multiplication facts probably in one setting because memorization was one of my strengths.

Having said that, at that age, I didn't understand how to leverage my strengths to tackle my weaknesses. God worked it out. After more losses, I finally got a win. By the time I became a senior, I had taken all of the required math courses to graduate, and I felt I could finally rest because I was on point with the rest of my curriculum.

I became more business-minded. I believed that one day I would become a business owner, so I launched out and signed up to take accounting as an elective. This was not a good experience for me either. However, this would not be the last time I would become an accounting student. I knew deep inside, I needed to redeem myself.

Growing up, I wanted to be both a school teacher and a business owner, and I had no idea that the gift of encouragement was brewing inside me. With my business goal in mind, I found myself focusing on the big picture as I continued to walk it out in faith and efforts, plugging in, diving in, and plunging in. Where would I find the opportunity to help someone? How would I ever get close when I had all these "missing the mark" experiences?

Despite the negative voices, I knew certain things in my youth that contributed to my positive traits. There was no doubt in my mind that I was a child of the King. God doesn't work magic tricks, but He's closer than any brother. I knew I had something in me that the world would need. I didn't know that the only way to bring it out was through defeats and disappointments. The most surprising thing was to realize that trauma would become my triumphant force.

WE ARE WINNERS

It is God's will for you and me to win, but that doesn't mean it will be easy. This means that if you follow His lead, ask for His help, and stay focused until the task is completed, you can succeed.

Whether you've heard it once or a hundred times, how you'll win your first battle is by winning the battle of the mind. If you overcome worries, doubts, confusion, anger, and feelings of defeat, you will be victorious even if you cannot see it immediately.

Those adolescent years can be challenging, but you learn so much that you should take into adulthood. One of my regrets is how much time and effort I wasted trying to keep up with everyone else. It is true that hindsight is 20-20. If I had known my true priorities, I would have put all my effort and time into developing her into the Gwen she would become.

Nothing is lost. In order to share wholeheartedly, I had to experience a few no-win situations. I wouldn't be able to mentor young ladies now if I hadn't taken some detours along the way. Somehow, I knew I was made for what I am doing now, managing my business, encouraging, and teaching. These three things I feel I could perform with my eyes closed. I had to be keenly aware that my steps were ordered by God, and I was made to put my best foot forward.

That's why I was so determined to get my next level of education. Love Letters from the MuM (LLFTM), my first book, tells the story of how I started college at the age of forty-two. It is for this reason that I was afraid the giants of my past would meet me there. Was my thinking correct? Yes, but I was ready this time. In addition to being covered in prayers by my husband and my biological family, I also was covered in prayers by my church family. It was God who was for me, so who could be against me?

Adulthood has a way of maturing you, and I believe I now know how to balance my life, so I do not take things too lightly, and likewise, I do not take things too seriously. I do not consider that to be an oxymoron. I conquered high school, technical school, and business school, but now it was time for me to live out one of my dreams. Age was not a factor. There were many who succeeded in college who were older when they started than me. Finding the right academic program was key. Once again, the Lord did not disappoint me.

BIRDS OF A FEATHER FLOCK TOGETHER

In my opinion, you become who you hang around. At the time, I was surrounded by African American women in leadership positions in my workplace. Many of them had graduate degrees. Those details really got me thinking. Those voices, the ones from fifth-grade, were still speaking. They were telling me that I wouldn't be able to do it. They told me that it was too challenging. The voices were saying things like, "Why do you want a degree? You already have a promising career." Those voices kept trying to talk me out of it. They were saying things like, "Put your energy into helping your husband complete his degree, and while you are at it, send your sons to college and leave the learning to them." These voices were caving in on me.

Again, I knew I was getting ready to shut the voices down. Having a made-up mind, stepping out on faith, and just doing it is how I gained my independence from the demons that tried to contain me. I asked myself, "What is the worst thing that could happen?" I accepted the risk and moved into my greatness.

At the time I entered college, I worked at the Defense Supply Center in Richmond, Virginia. We occasionally hosted education fairs for colleges. I saw a flyer in the cafeteria announcing Averett University's visit. I remember vividly placing the flyer at the back of my calendar. I missed the event, but I meditated on the possibility. I fought doubt and fear all the way, but I made up my mind that I was going on a field trip to visit them.

In talking to my supervisor, I shared my short-term and long-term goals, and she pushed me even further. As soon as I picked up the phone, I contacted Averett University and booked an appointment to speak with a counselor. It was the first victory, but it wasn't the last.

I knew that all testimonies begin with a test. This was truly my test of faith. The decision to start college at forty-two was not a mistake, a fluke, or a waste of time. After I felt confident that my foundation was solid, I allowed myself to be challenged, and I conquered the negative vibes of fear that had kept me stuck for so long. Except for the girl in the mirror, I wasn't trying to prove anything to anyone. As a student, my confidence would be boosted to the level it would need to be to become an encourager, a business owner, and a teacher. That's what I wanted to be.

Lacking the mental strength to cut through distractions is one thing, but the feeling that you cannot learn or maintain focus is another. Having the ability to concentrate properly as well as winning the war on procrastination are achievements that call for celebration. Believe me, I celebrate every victory.

You never fully appreciate a victory until you experience a few defeats, but even in periods of defeat, keep your cool. There was a commercial years ago advertising deodorant with the tagline, "Never let them see you sweat." Those are my sentiments exactly! Never let your enemy or your opposition penalize you for unsportsmanlike conduct.

SEASON OF PROCESS

During one of my times of defeat in my career, I knew the Lord blessed me with this particular position. It was not an everyday opportunity. It was an answer to my prayer. However, I struggled in the workplace like never before. You probably can guess in the end, it was a blessing. The challenges I experienced provided me with

GWENDOLYN CODY-DAVIS

so many life lessons. I will refer to this season as "a season of process."

I have noticed that many people desire blessings, and what everyone really wants is the testimony of God opening huge doors. If we told the whole story, the world would know that occasionally once you enter the open doors, the difficulties of the task diminish the desire of the dream. For years, I blamed the enemy for everything bad that happened to me until I realized I had to own up to my shortcomings. Once I took responsibility, stopped blaming others even if it was in my mind, and stopped dwelling on what went wrong, I began to focus on how I could course correct and make the proper adjustments.

After praying, meditating, and talking to my husband, it occurred to me that every failure placed me closer to success. In my government and private sector career, I never received a bad evaluation; however, this particular season taught me a valuable lesson about me. I began to see opportunities for personal growth, and I embraced them. My strategy for overcoming defeat has been to set new goals. Occasionally, there will be road bumps along the way. Nevertheless, the Lord helped me to move past them, which helped me to focus on new goals instead.

Another revelation I received recently was to be careful how you hear information. Although we must listen in order to receive information, we must be careful about how we hear it. I found that concept to be life-changing for me. One bad word or bad vibe from the wrong person can ruin your entire day if you allow it. Maybe the information was not meant to be negative, but you heard it in a negative or threatening way. Sometimes, you have to examine yourself and the space you're in.

DISTRACTIONS

We live in the age of information. I remember when you had to wait on the daily newspaper for the news or as some will call it, the "tea." You would have to wait for your favorite magazine to hit the newsstand or your mailbox before you could get the inside scoop, but those days are gone forever.

Social media platforms have replaced the six-o'clock news. The answers to any questions you may have are only a click away on your digital device. Cell phones are now used to run businesses. These things are great and necessary. There is only one problem; we are constantly distracted. Unfortunately, many of our mobile devices serve more as distractions than as tools for helping us. We can benefit from the tools we have to help us, but keep in mind, they also can hurt us.

It's important to always know your priorities. Your journey displays your strengths and weaknesses. It's not all uphill, but adversities help you achieve goals, which should motivate you to never give up. I always encourage others to be great and inspire others to do likewise. Confirm that you are aligned with Father God's blueprint for your life. His blueprint is His Word. Allow your goals to be the center of your attention. Whatever is in the center will be the focus of what you hone in on.

According to the old saying, "Nothing beats a failure more than a try." When you are preparing for greatness, equipping yourself is not a sin. Helping someone will require you to go through certain things, and sometimes, those things are unpleasant. Since your purpose is much bigger than you, and your heart is encouraging, you see life events in a positive light and realize it all has been worth it.

YOU CAN WIN THE MENTAL BATTLE

Mind battles are real battles. You should not go through them alone. Seeking counsel from your pastor, spiritual leader, accountability partner, or a therapist to share your mind battles is strongly advised. We are not made to live isolated lives, especially when we are going through difficult times.

The Lord is good at surprises. Every time I feel discouraged, He goes out of His way to have someone reach out to me whom I least expect. He does it on purpose, and He does it with a purpose. In times of despair, I believe it is only the testing of my faith that causes me to hear a small still voice that provides encouragement. The process is similar to refueling at a gas station. As soon as I fill up I make positive deposits in others. We all need to refuel at times and become more authentically laser-focused. How can you do that? Have a "me" moment. For just a moment, everything revolves around you. As you examine your intentions, can you see yourself expanding your territory? If you answered yes, visualize yourself growing in wisdom and faith every day. It is okay to look back and reflect on the past, but keep your eyes on the prize. Let your life become a living witness. This will send a signal to others that you are faith-filled and unstoppable. Make certain you get the proper rest and nurture your mind, body and soul.

If you seek advice from others, which is not a sign of weakness but a sign of humility, then you will see the glass as half full rather than half empty. A positive outlook on life sets the tone. In order to advance from one step to the next, you need as many optimists as you can accommodate. It might be one person. Remember, you and God are the majority if you're a believer.

There is no one person alive who has not experienced, at one time or another, feelings of defeat and failure, but that should not be how your story ends because you are an overcomer.

Below, I offer seven strategies to help you overcome failures. Apply them and know you are no longer blocked and no longer stopped.

✓ Accept feelings and emotions — It is healthy to acknowledge your feelings rather than hide them. There is very little you can do to avoid disappointments and failures. When you realize life goes on, you make the necessary adjustments within your control. Experiences of defeat can serve as a powerful testimony as well as fuel your energy to join the "I will never give up community."

✓ Knowing that failure does not mean your life is going to be over — I couldn't digest what was happening to me when I was in fifth-grade. I thought that feeling of defeat would follow me for the rest of my life, but it didn't. Facing my giants and conquering my fears head on helped me overcome the scars and the shame. Truth be told, we all experience the mountaintop highs and the valley lows. However, how could you truly offer assistance to someone else in a similar situation if you never hit the valley lows?

✓ Learn from failures and be constructive — What about your lessons learned? Isn't learning how to become better the overall goal? Consider the question: How can you position yourself constructively and not destructively?

Your failures help you encourage someone.

Your failures build your character.

Your failures help you to become more determined.

Your failures actually help make you more of a positive person.

Your failures help turn your attitude into the little engine that could.

✓ Find inspiration — Be your own inspirational speaker. Read, write, or speak something inspiring on a daily basis. Make it a practice to find someone and something that inspires you.

✓ Don't give up — Keep trying with all your best efforts. It has been said that every "no" brings you closer to a "yes." How will you allow the "no's" to affect you when Father God has plenty of open doors. His promises are yes and yes.

✓ Surround yourself with positive people — Not only that, surround yourself with people who give you life. An old English proverb says, "Birds of a feather flock together." In my personal experience, I have found that when you surround yourself with positive thinking, you are more likely to focus on your objectives. It makes you feel empowered to succeed and be energized and motivated.

✓ You are blessed to be a blessing — Accept the fact that your life journey is not all about you. It's about the people who God places on your path to love, to nurture, to speak life, and to provide a godly example.

I have been taught from one of the prayers of St. Teresa of Avila:
"Christ has no body now on earth but yours,
no hands but yours,
no feet but yours,
Yours are the eyes through which to look out
Christ's compassion to the world
Yours are the feet with which he is to go about
doing good;
Yours are the hands with which he is to bless men
now."

GWENDOLYN CODY-DAVIS

T   H   R   E   E

Keep The Dream Alive

"Without execution, your dream is just a nap."
—*John Jennings*

What things have you always wanted to do? Where have you always wanted to visit? If you were born between the years of 1946-1964, you are classified as a baby boomer. I love asking these questions especially to my peers. I have met some baby boomers who believe that the process of pursuing dreams is over at age fifty. I am shocked and appalled. Where did that energy originate?

IT'S YOUR CHOICE

We make daily choices on our journey. Either we work towards our dreams, or we continue dreaming. Does it take hard work? Yes, it does. Do you have to wake up and realize that it takes you to turn your dream into reality? Yes, you do. I have always been a dreamer. Dreams motivate me to keep pressing forward. They always give me something to anticipate. Dreaming is only the first step in moving to your next level. However, without a plan of execution, a dream remains a dream.

I received a prophetic word from my bishop, Charles E. Wiley, Sr., that I would be an author, and that prophecy resulted in my first book. I began to dream about becoming an author. While I had some idea of what it would entail, it wasn't until I actually did the work and stepped into the role that I saw the dream manifest, and I knew how it felt to birth a book.

The key phrase is that I had to put in the work. I had to make mistakes. I had sleepless nights. I sometimes wished I had not even begun the project. I wanted to quit. It felt too difficult at times, and I wanted to crawl into a hole and just cry.

Once I realized I wasn't the only author who suffered these kinds of things, I accepted that this was part of the process. That's why it's not a good idea to isolate yourself when God gives you an assignment. You will need help. The thought of being alone on life's journey is absurd anyway.

EXECUTING THE DREAM IS THE ISSUE

I have found that when I meet people and hear their stories, they have no problem dreaming. For some, it's just as natural as breathing. While they have ideas, plans, hopes, and wishes, executing the dream is the challenge. You cannot allow the dream to overwhelm you because you'll stall even more.

I experienced great success in my first coaching program, which guided me through my first two books. However, when that door closed, the question welled up inside of me, "What do you do when your well runs dry?" The answer that came to me was to look for other opportunities. Having the faith and the growth mindset to move on is important; you must trust that God is leading you. Why not go ahead and bet on yourself?

Sometimes, when a door closes, we extend ourselves and do something we would not do ordinarily. We go through many stages of seeing our dreams come to pass. It may begin as a wish and hope and then materialize to a strong desire. Once it becomes a strong desire, you can feel it in your spirit. Your emotions are intertwined with it, and you won't stop until you reach your goal.

When I felt led to write this book, I prayed and researched a coaching program that would be ideal for me. I sought a coaching program with the mentality of our older son, who used to write "no days off" on his t-shirts. With that mindset, I sought a coaching program that would propel, and challenge me to birth my best work. I have a saying, "What I don't know will make a whole world [of difference]." I am learning so much about my industry as an author and as a rising inspirational and motivational coach. Yet, this information and guidance did not just fall from the sky. I made an investment to acquire the success I am expecting to enjoy. That is my recommendation for you. To see a dream come to fruition, seek God's Word to receive God's win. Don't be afraid to move out on what He places on your heart. Unless I sought mentorship and had a made-up mind, nothing could have happened.

As I reflect on my first book, I dreamed of writing it before I knew what I would write. I dreamed of people reading and enjoying it. While I was wise enough to know that some people would like it, and some people would not like it, I had to decide if I would allow the outliers to discourage me. No way. Regardless of whether it was written for one person or helped one person, I was willing to take the chance of sharing my experience and God's love to help people overcome their fears, failures, and faults.

I believe everyone dreams. I also believe people know that in order to see that dream become a reality, they have to have an action plan. While there may not be an expiration date on dreams, you must place an execution date on the plans. Are you feeling that I am encouraging you to pursue your dream? Yes, I am. No matter your age, you should never stop dreaming. Who told you that your dream is irrelevant? Who told you that your dream would never come to pass? Who told you that your dream is not worth pursuing?

TO SHARE OR NOT TO SHARE?

Be careful of negative vibes. Be careful of the naysayers. Be careful with whom you share your dreams. Some will be unable to handle them, and some will not be able to handle you. I believe in God-given dreams. With my God-given faith, I have decided to make every strong attempt to carry it out. After seeing one dream come true, I work incredibly on the next one. They never stop with me. I have so many dreams, and I feel like I'm just getting started.

IF YOU ONLY CAN SEE IT, YOU CAN ACHIEVE IT

When I was a child, my mom subscribed to House Beautiful magazine. I looked forward to receiving those magazines in the mail each month. When I got them out of the mailbox, I would smile, read them, and visualize how I wanted my environment to look. I would dream, dream, and dream some more. I dreamed of having a nice house, a nice yard, and a grand décor that I could make using my creativity and the magazine pictures as a starter base. Those magazines started as visuals. Years before Pinterest was created officially, I started my own private Pinterest by cutting out pictures from magazines and making my own designs. It became a hobby at the time. When I wasn't playing with my Barbies and my dollhouses, I was creating these home designs and longing to live in a nice modern house.

I remember every house we lived in as a military family. In Belgium, we lived in two homes, and I decorated the second one so nicely. The décor was European-American modern from the 1980s. All of my decorating ideas came from my self-made Pinterest boards, which, little did I know, showed that I was a visionary.

When we moved back to the states, we lived in a nice apartment for three years before purchasing our very first home. It was, however, a shared dream of my husband and me to become homeowners. It was an exciting time for us. The first home we bought was a townhouse in Bowie, Maryland. What a grand experience! We lived in that home for six years.

Every negative voice in the universe traveled to inform us that we would not be able to afford a home in that area. Keep in mind, the negative voices were not real people, just negative vibes, doubt, fear, and maybe every now and then, someone might give us that okay look.

Initially, my husband did not want to look at houses because he did not want to be disappointed. The voices of the naysayers, even just in his head, would say, "Are you kidding me right now?" You're an E-7 in the U.S. Army, and even though it's just you and your wife, you love to travel, drive European cars like Audis and Saabs, shop at Louis Vuitton, and eat at expensive restaurants. You can never afford to own a home in this high-cost area. We listened to the voices for a short time, but then we got that victorious feeling, and suddenly, we were all in. We realized we could accomplish this dream if we worked together, and we did.

Every time God allows us to do something big, he always places the right people around us. At that time, we were members of Shiloh Baptist Church in Landover Maryland under the leadership of the late Pastor Paul P. Pitchford. We soon discovered Shiloh was a loving and giving ministry. It was here we first learned about giving God His tithe. We also learned that the church contained all the wisdom and expertise needed to fulfill any dream possible. Our realtor was a member of Shiloh. The Lord knew that as first-time homeowners, we needed a super realtor. God sent us such a person who helped us get our finances in order to be eligible to purchase our first home. We were in our home within ninety days of our first meeting with our realtor. It was like gravy. God gave us the desire; we dreamed the dream. We visualized the house. We sought wise counsel, and the results manifested.

As I shared with a girlfriend recently, even though we celebrate birthdays annually, we are aging every second of the day. Each day we wake up is a victory. That is exactly why you don't want to place a dream on layaway and never return to claim it. You have to have a made-up mind that no matter what you're going through, you're not going to bend or break until you see your dream come true.

As previously stated, be aware that dream killers do exist. Perhaps these are people who have given up on their dreams. Maybe they lack the aggressiveness, or maybe they are not willing to put the work into their dreams. As a result, they find it impossible to encourage your aspirations.

These are the same people who will try to talk you out of your purpose, your assignment, and your mission. This is why they are called dream killers. Be forewarned. Ask God for wisdom when it comes to the people with whom you share your dreams and remember that the good news is that God will send the right kind of help.

Guard your dream as you guard your heart. Visualize your dreams becoming reality. You cannot afford any more delays or excuses. Who plans to fail? Not you. Plan to succeed and encourage every coachable dreamer you meet. The reason you need to execute your dream is because dreams are what, I'm sure, keep you inspired and motivated. It's important to keep the dream alive and know that dreams help keep you alive. Having a dream and turning the dream into a reality is not easy, but you cannot be willing to just do what is "easy."

Sometimes, finding the starting place is challenging especially if you're the type of person who has many interests. I have learned from many wise leaders to find your niche and then work on your dream from there. Finding your purpose is just as important as tapping into your dream.

You have to be a lot like an athlete who visualizes winning the game at all costs. Develop the mindset that your dream has to come to fruition. I am so excited about your dream and your ability to keep it alive. I encourage you to own your dream and execute it without delay, no more intermission and no more excuses.

USE YOUR MEASURE OF FAITH TO ACCOMPLISH YOUR DREAMS

Perhaps you are not the type of person who has the self-confidence to pursue your dream. The first step is to recognize past achievements. Did you celebrate your past victories? Keep in mind that we all have gifts and strengths. What may seem effortless to one person may be another person's struggle. Finding out what you do well is the most important thing for you. That's usually the gift you are blessed with to bless others. All of us have been given a measure of faith, according to Romans 12:3b, and along with that, we all have the capacity in which to deal with life's issues. As for my faith, I like to refer to it as a "whole measure of faith," and you have a "whole measure of faith" too. With that whole measure of faith, you can turn your dreams into realities.

Another issue we sometimes face is self-acceptance. We tend to be more critical of our weaknesses and imperfections. No one is asking you to be a perfect person. Accept yourself for who you are and be willing to make improvements along the way. If you accept who you are, knowing that you are unique and creative, you will be empowered and full of gratitude, and you most likely will move out in the directions of your dreams. Dreams should not to be taken lightly, but instead, they should be viewed as a gateway to a better life. Sometimes, dreams help us find our way in life. That's why it's important to hold fast to your dreams.

Another discovery is to know the danger of comparing yourself to others. When you compare yourself to others, you are insulting your God-given uniqueness. It never pays to do that. Comparisons between people is a recipe for constant frustration. There is always someone who will be better than you in certain areas. Cheer them on and move on with your own gifts, talents and abilities.

WRITE DOWN THE VISION

How do you move from being a dreamer to a masterful dream executor? I highly suggest understanding your assignment and setting realistic goals. Do not be afraid of setting goals that will allow you to frame your world successfully. I write my short-term and long-term goals for the week, the month, the quarter, and the year. Sure, dreams float around in your head, but it's best to write them down. It's better for me to visualize them quarterly. That way it seems realistically reachable. Biting off more than you can chew will lead to failure, and another unexecuted dream will go down the drain.

One of my favorite scriptures is Habakkuk 2:2-3. This passage informs you to "Write down the vision; write it clearly on clay tables so whoever reads it can run to tell others. It is not yet time for the message to come true, but that time is coming soon; the message will come true. It may seem like a long time, but be patient and wait for it, because it will surely come; it will not be delayed."

If the vision needs not to be delayed, neither should you. You need a strong sense of commitment. Staying committed may mean having an accountability partner. Even if that partnership does not work out, hold yourself accountable. Shortcuts at this point only will rob you. The community you are assigned to bless also will be impacted. You need to be able to see the goal and track your progress. It could be as simple as making a checklist and checking things off as you go.

I learned this process years ago when I was a Mary Kay consultant, but the concept works with everything. Recently, I heard a podcast episode about a lady who was so impressed with a checklist that she completed a couple of tasks that she hadn't included on her list. However, she added them in just so she could check them off. This is clever, especially if you want to chart your progress accurately. I am that person. I do the very same thing. I need to see progress. If not, I will lose heart. Have you ever noticed the gleam in the eyes of a person who just graduated from high school, trade school, college, basic training or achieved a milestone?

The gleam represents, I finished what I started, and I am proud of myself.

Finishing what you started is a skill. Think about it. Finishing the projects that you started speaks volumes about your character. Your sense of achievement and confidence is heightened. Finishing what you started despite all the odds shows you are trustworthy, self-assured, self-reliant, confident, and capable of being true to your word. As parents, we repeatedly told our sons, "If you start it, you need to finish it." Commitment has to be developed, and the sooner that we develop it, the better. If you quit because it got too hard, what will be said of your life as you keep living? If you quit because you ran into trouble, take the advice given in Proverbs 24:10, which tells you that giving up when trouble comes shows that we are weak. You don't want it to be said that you started many tasks and projects (got distracted, frustrated, doubtful, or fearful) but finished nothing. Being uncommitted has consequences. Your lack of commitment will manifest itself in your relationships, your employment, and yes, even in the execution of your dreams.

Growing up, I was a Brownie and later a Girl Scout. I was so excited about serving in that capacity. When I was old enough to be a Girl Scout, I had even a deeper commitment to the organization. My scout meetings were at 4:30 p.m. every week at St. Thomas African Methodist Episcopal Church, less than a mile away from my house, but as a child, it seemed so far away, especially when I had to walk; the meetings occurred before my parents got off work.

I took the Scout commitment even further. My mom sometimes chaperoned weekend events in which we participated and earned badges. My younger sister, Tangela, also became a Brownie when she was old enough to join. As a big sister, I was happy to chaperone her on her Brownie trips. I learned five essential skills from my scouting experience: goal setting, money management, people skills, decision-making, and business ethics. Who knew these skills would set me up for life? How committed are you to your future goals?

Being fully committed simply means making a choice that you do not mind being inconvenienced temporarily for a permanent positive outcome. The worst thing to do is to make excuses. It's too easy. We usually are not in the most blessed position when things are too easy. Recently, I learned a new term from my coach. You have to invest in "sweat equity." Eventually, you realize that you would do it again if you could repeat the experience of that level of success.

COMMIT TO YOUR GOALS

In order to crush your goals, always remember successful goal achievement requires one hundred percent commitment. Distractions don't pack up and leave just because you are working on a goal; however, make sure you possess a high level of commitment. If you have the mind to do it, watch out world. You will get it done. Additionally, it's important to remember to give yourself grace when things aren't going as well as you would like.

One of the greatest stories of commitment for me comes from the Word of God. The story unfolds in Genesis 11:4 concerning the dramatic events of the Tower of Babel. Funny thing is that their commitment level was great, but their focus and overall goal was all wrong. The people were not following God's instructions, but rather, they were creating their own path outside God's will. There is one place you do not want to be, and that is outside God's will.

As a Bible student, you probably know that at that time in history, there was not a need for a Rosetta Stone;

the entire world spoke the same language. Nevertheless, the people decided to build a city with a tower, but this tower would reach up to heaven. There was no question that the people were skilled in construction. They were capable of getting the work done, but the problem was the purpose of the project. Truthfully, their purpose was to make themselves famous to prevent the population from being scattered across the Earth.

The word, Babel, means "to confuse." God observed how powerful the people's unity of purpose was. God, in His infinite wisdom, knew this project only would lead to the people's separation from Him, so He purposely confused their language, causing them to speak many different languages. By doing so, they would not understand each other. By doing this, God opposed the people's attempt. He also forced the people of the city to scatter all across the face of the Earth. From this story, we learn that when unity and purpose show up on the scene, anything can be accomplished. Despite it being the wrong purpose, Divine intervention in human affairs was necessary. God made it clear that man would not overstep His limitations.

Make sure you are in God's plan before you utilize your energy on any project. Tap into His power by prayer and meditation to get the results you need. As you are aware, Rome was not built in a day, so your dream will not manifest overnight. In the end, stick-to-itiveness works. Positive mindsets work. Once you put in the work, you can make dreams come true. Don't be afraid to ask for help. Again, God will send the right kind of help. Whatever you do, don't give up.

Can you visualize your desired outcome? When I had my photoshoot done for this book cover and book promotions, I was in a very chic location. I made a statement to a person on my photographer's team that I could see myself conducting workshops there. I imagined it like I was already conducting the presentation. I just felt it. I could see it. Just by making that declaration, I was pointed in the direction of someone who could help me. Vision is very important in accomplishing goals. I am convinced that if you can see it, you can achieve it. Can you be trusted with a vision?

During college, I remember gazing out my bedroom window especially on Saturday mornings in the summer and seeing neighbors preparing for beach trips, weddings, and all kinds of occasions. I would long to be a part of something fun besides homework. My husband reminded me, "But look at what you are doing." You are changing your future one class at a time. That was exactly what I needed to hear to help build my momentum to keep going. Ever since that season of my life, I have been motivated to inspire others. If you've tried and failed in past commitments, shake it off quickly. The past is the past, and you are a different person with each experience. Believe in your heart that you are armed with the strength and the tools you need to execute your dreams successfully. Focusing on the end result instead of momentary temptation will help you make the right choices that will support your desired outcome.

In Psalm 37:5, the Bible encourages us to depend on the Lord, to trust Him, and to be at ease with Him; He will take care of you. Respect your goals, dreams, and aspirations. It may appear that someone is moving much faster than you. It still does not diminish your efforts. It does not dismiss your dream. The key is for you to give it your best shot. You aren't competing with anyone else but yourself in reality. I love the saying that a flower doesn't think of competing with other flowers. It just blooms, and that's how you will feel when you execute your dreams.

FOUR

Next Level Integrity

*"The good people who live honest lives will be a blessing
to their children."*

—*Proverbs 20:7*

Have you ever wondered if the word, "integrity," is still in the English language or in any language? It seems that doing the right thing is no longer emphasized. The emphasis is on doing what you want to do, regardless of whether it's right or wrong.

Who wakes up in the morning with wrong thoughts or actions in their minds? According to the news, too many people operate this way, and the things we see happening all around us confirm it. Core values are one of the most critical ingredients missing in our world today. Simply stated core values are the qualities of honesty and morality when every opportunity is met with integrity and the desire to do the right thing.

EMBRACE CORE VALUES

There were times in my younger life when I did not always cling to the core values I was taught. I recall one of those times just before I got married. I worked at an insurance company in Atlanta, Georgia, and I decided to not give a two-week notice. I just quit. My reasoning was that I would collect my last paycheck at break time and leave at lunch for the rest of the day. At the time, it sounded like a good idea. Meanwhile, I moved out of my apartment and moved in with a friend. I didn't think my plan through; since I didn't return after lunch, my employer got worried. Only one person at work knew about my plan, but one person was all it took.

My employer and colleagues were aware that I was engaged, but they didn't know that I was leaving Atlanta and moving to Ghlin, Belgium. The following week, my supervisor called my parents' home number; I panicked when they asked to speak to me, and I handed the phone to my grandmother. I mouthed the answers to my employer's questions to her. She covered for me. She informed them that I was not there, but that she would give me the message to call them back.

My grandmother did this out of an act of love to

protect me. She had not been forewarned; she simply winged it. I was relieved.

In hindsight, I regret this experience, and I have never duplicated it. Since I skipped out on the exit meeting, the company for whom I worked needed to tie up some things with me, and they handled it in a professional manner. I did not. I had nothing to fear; however, if I had operated in full integrity, I would not have put my grandmother through that ordeal. I would not have gone through it myself. Because of my greed, I thought they were going to hold my last paycheck. I was so wrong.

Operating in integrity does not mean you always will get it right. Trust and believe, there are times you will not. However, it does mean you will do your best to remain honest, dependable, and respectful. I realize that when you're an honest person, you always can be yourself. There is no need to think about how you will cover up the next lie. You do not need to worry about what you told one person and what you need to say the next time. The truth is always the truth.

The truth is that we do not see core values consistently displayed in our communities. Growing up, I remember that keeping your promises made you a trustworthy person. When you kept your word, you were considered credible. Many business relationships began in that way, and you may remember the simple gesture of shaking hands symbolized good faith, trust, and loyalty. Signing a document or signing a contract did not always mean we were in business. A handshake signified bonds and a commitment to do the right thing.

In my opinion, core values should never go out of style. But, if they are not taught to and emulated constantly, they will go right out the window. What do you have if you don't have core values? Core values are fundamental beliefs of a person or organization. What will assist you in developing your guiding principles without core values? Principles dictate behavior and help you understand the difference between correct and incorrect behavior.

Core values help set priorities, and they can be used to help you answer questions on how to measure your life and if things are going the way you planned. Ultimately, it is up to you to determine your core value system.

STAND ON TRUTH

As a child of God, we cannot overlook His characteristics. The first thing to remember is that God is one hundred percent truth. God does not play April Fool's jokes. His Word provides His history and His promises. He will do exactly what He says He will do. Find yourself in His Word. When you are God-conscious, words like holy, good, just, impartial, infinite, and patient make you immediately think of our loving Father. In setting spiritual growth goals for myself, my daily prayer is to be more like Him. In order for others to see God in me, I want to operate in integrity like He does.

I don't just want to be like Him for others to think I'm this super spiritual person. Not at all. My ultimate goal is to please God. My journey has been long enough that I know if my ways please Him, my heart's desires are met. Who wouldn't want to be right and walk upright before Him? I once said I wanted to be like God, but I really didn't know what I was saying. I had not reached the part of my spiritual journey where God's Word trumped everything. It wasn't until my late twenties that I realized what it meant to sell out completely to God even though I gave my heart to the Lord at age eight.

Many Christians, however, think if you go to church and look the part that you are okay. Nevertheless, your efforts should reflect your desire to strive for improvements and to become more spiritually alert. In the past, I would attend church services and maybe volunteer to do something in the ministry to make people think I was spiritual. That worked for a while, but deep down, you know if you're living the truth or living a lie. If it's the truth, you keep striving for the truth. Living a lie means keeping plenty of lies in your immediate environment because you never know when you will have to use them. Nevertheless, if you're not operating in truth, you aren't displaying God's attributes, and if you're not displaying God's attributes, who are you representing?

As previously stated, being perfect is not something we can attain, and this is not what it means to be like God. If God knew (and He did), that we could be perfect, then why did he give us His Son and His Spirit to help us in our imperfections? Oh yes, we need His help. We have all the tools necessary to operate in integrity and be godly. Being like God simply means to follow God's examples.

Ask yourself the questions below, and if there is any deficit, how can you position yourself to get better? My recommendations on how to operate on a higher level of integrity as it pertains to each question, follows.

Can you keep information confidential?
If someone confides in you, can you keep it to yourself? What if the boot was on the other foot? If you placed the utmost trust in someone enough to share a problem or something of a personal nature, would you want it exposed? I don't think so. When it comes to not sharing a personal, confidential matter with others, can you upgrade? If you're not the person for the assignment, please let the person know that you are not a secret keeper. One of the most hurtful things you can do to someone is to announce their critical information to the world. You only have to mention it to one person, and no one has any control over where that information will end. You have to be wise enough to be a real confidant. What if you're the only person in whom someone wants to confide? Will you discipline yourself to be loyal enough to operate in integrity?

Leaders always should be sensitive to personal information to which they are privy, whether it comes from their employees or church members. It is so important to not only be honest, well-grounded, and authentic but also a leader is considered to be dependable and trustworthy. As a result of past betrayals, people who need to share will not share.

Can you admit when you are wrong?
Simply own it, admit it, and if need be, apologize for any misunderstandings. Be ready to move on. There will be other opportunities to make God a proud parent.

Can you avoid gossip at all costs?
Gossip comes in many forms, but it always leads to strife. Being surrounded by strife-filled situations is not living your best life. Make a conscious decision to live in a no strife zone.

Can you keep a promise?
Remember that a promise is a promise. Follow through on the things you said you would do. Usually, people don't want to look as though they have dropped the ball, leaving others in awkward situations because they didn't keep their word. You and I are not without flaws, but make your word mean something. I remember my

grandmother saying, "Let your word always be your balm." Allow your core values to take shape and make a huge difference in the world.

GWENDOLYN CODY-DAVIS

F I V E

Laughter Is Like A Medicine With No Side Effects

"He who laughs last, laughs best."
— John Heywood

Have you ever laughed so hard that you cried? I have. Laughter is good for the soul, so I choose it on a daily basis. I love to laugh. I love the way it makes me feel; I love its sound and the unexpected, uncontrollable, and infectious nature of it. We have God's approval to laugh. He even does it Himself! High-spirited, cheerful people who appreciate the power of a laugh are gleeful, light-hearted, and joyful. I am convinced that laughter is a valuable tool to help balance life.

WHERE THERE IS LAUGHTER, THERE IS HOPE

My dad passed away in January 2001. After my family and I made arrangements at the funeral home, a spirit of laughter broke out of nowhere. We were walking up the street to the florist shop when someone said something that sent us all into a hearty belly laugh. Although I can't remember what was said or who said it, I will never forget how we laughed and laughed together. Laughter turned moments of sadness into gladness.

How timely that moment was! To me, laughter is a gift. If you have ever lost a loved one, and somehow, in the midst of all of the planning of a life celebration, you can find laughter, you have found a reason to keep pressing forward. In life, it's important to have a good sense of humor. Life is not a bowl of cherries, and no one is on top of the world every day. Laughter is powerful, especially on the not-so-good days; it helps you relax, breathe, and enjoy your journey.

Ecclesiastes 3:4 says there is a time to cry and a time to laugh. My hope is that you never miss out on your time to laugh. As we reflect on current world events, we must remind ourselves not to take life too seriously, even though we take the events to heart. One of the ways

Christians show the world who we are is through our joy. Joy is a fruit of the Holy Spirit, and what better way is there to express joy than through laughter?

Laughter is great for the soul, and I have seen laughter get someone out of trouble. My paternal grandmother, Marie Cody, lived with us, and she was not only our granny: she was also a live-in babysitter, chef, and housekeeper. She did all these jobs well, but she wasn't good at disciplining her granddaughters, my sister Tangela and me. She was way too soft.

Although our parents were the primary disciplinarians, our grandmother attempted to step up her game when they were not around. Let's just say she was too emotionally attached, and my sister and I still laugh about it to this very day. When Tangela got in trouble with our grandmother, she would say, "Gwen, get me a switch." As a child, if you had to choose your own weapon or your siblings' weapon, you'd choose the lightest, least intimidating switch you could find. Whenever I would go out in the front yard and look for a switch, my sister would start running, and my grandmother would tell me to catch her. By the time I did this, all three of us were laughing so hard, the spanking was off, out of reach, and in other words, canceled. It turned into more of a group hug than anything. I now realize those were special times of bonding that we will cherish forever. What if the people in the world would lay down their weapons, have a group hug, and just laugh?

WHEN YOU LAUGH, THE WORLD LAUGHS WITH YOU

There are so many benefits to laughing, and one of my favorites is that it reduces stress. Medical science says laughter produces chemicals in the body that not only relieve stress, but they also enhance people's physical and mental health. Medical science was not the first to make this discovery. The Bible mentioned this long before man discovered it. With our lives seeming to be pressure-filled every single second, who couldn't use a laugh or two? Laughter helps boost our immune systems. Laugher also can be contagious.

King Solomon is recorded in the Bible as the wisest man. His powerful proverbs are words for Christians to use to guide their lives even in the twenty-first century. According to Proverbs 17:22, a happy heart is like good medicine, but a broken spirit drains your strength. Laughing not only feels good, but it is good for you. This "medicine" is fast and free, and it can be taken anywhere in the universe. In addition to offering benefits to your physical health, laughter benefits your mental and emotional well-being, and again it helps you cope with the stresses of everyday life.

Hanging out with friends is usually a sure way that laughter will be served. Early in our marriage, my husband and I hosted many football parties. It started with playoff games and the Super Bowl, but it quickly evolved into weekly regular season games of the National Football League (NFL). We would host one week, and then another couple would host the next week and so on. It went around to probably three or four families. Even those who didn't understand the game well came to our football brunches for the food, drinks, fellowship, and the laughter. We served enough laughter to last all week. Although we lived in Maryland at the time, wintertime weather had no effect on attendance. Our friends would come out in the rain, cold, and snow to hang out and watch our favorite sport. You can believe there was always laughter galore. The purpose of our get-togethers was to have a great time.

One of the most profound sights to experience is the smile and the laughter of a newborn baby. I remember our son's first smiles. In my opinion, it was a smile of appreciation. Even though babies cannot speak, I believe their smiles say, "Thanks for all you do."

Laughter is universal, and it can be found in a variety of places: your home, your job, your church, and your community. The key is to find it. Finding humor in everyday life can certainly lighten your life and help you see things in a different light. Again, whatever you do for yourself to reduce stress and improve your circumstances places you in the "W" column. Sometimes, when you read the side effects of a prescribed medication, you will find that the side effects can be more harmful than the condition that caused you to need the medicine. In spite of that, I am convinced there are no side effects to worry about when you use laughter as your primary medicine.

EXPERIENCE THE LIGHTER BRIGHTER SIDE OF LIFE

Keep in mind there is a bright side to life. One of the ways you can testify to this truth is to tap into joy. A lot of things are out of our control. Sometimes, we feel like just letting those things go. However, the things we can control should be handled with care, grace, and laughter.

Ideally, I would love to be known as an encourager. I feel like this is my life's mission. When I was a young girl, I was an encourager, and I didn't even realize what the gift was. I also would like to be known for my ability to laugh on purpose and spread love, joy and peace every place I enter. It would be wonderful if I could leave a legacy of love and laughter.

Listed below are three powerful tips about laughter that are proven to deliver.

√ Laugher offers some powerful health benefits to smile about.

It literally feels wonderful to laugh. I cannot emphasize it enough, when you laugh, you release what are known as endorphins or good chemicals. As endorphins are released, they improve your mood as well as increase your body's natural painkilling response. Extra endorphins give you a little lift necessary to feel good about your life. In my experience, laughter is a valuable coping mechanism that works every time you are stressed to max.

√ Remember, it is better to chuckle than to struggle.

Adding laughter is easier than you think. If you start by watching a funny TV show or movie, you will laugh. That's why comedies were created. Whether it's your favorite stand-up comedian or actor, as long as you find the humor and as long as no one gets hurt, it should work.

✓ Serve laughter with a meal or snack.

Would you prefer to curl up with your favorite snack and watch your favorite comedy show or worry yourself into a tizzy about things that may never happen? Our oldest son, Ryan, is almost five years to the day older than his younger brother, Reagan. When they were growing up, the dinner table was the place to converse about our day. As with most families, we shared the day's highlights over dinner before they were old enough to have extracurricular activities after school.

Having dinner together was the time when we would share jokes, or maybe one of us told a story that was not really funny, but the way it was delivered was the icing on the cake. There is no doubt it brightened everyone's day. I tell young parents all the time to value those precious years and moments because time is moving us constantly from one chapter to the next.

While we don't have a pet of our own, watching videos and looking at pictures of our grand pup, Lilly, brings my husband and me tons of laughs. We usually receive them at just the right time. We find that it is nice to be rejuvenated by the simple things in life.

GWENDOLYN CODY-DAVIS

S I X

Identity Crisis
Do Not Allow Anyone
To Define You

*"Before I made you in your mother's womb, I chose you. Before
you were born, I set you apart for a special work. I appointed
you as a prophet to the nations."*

—Jeremiah 1:5

Have you ever heard the expression "I don't look like what I've gone through?" In other words, if you only knew of my challenges, my triggers, and even my tears through my smiles, you wouldn't believe my story. Your personal life is your business, and you cannot share everything with everyone. I get that. Though holding your head high, compartmentalizing, and pressing forward is something you have to train yourself to do.

Growing up, there was a television show called *To Tell the Truth*. There were four celebrity panelists on the show and three contestants, two of whom were imposters. The host would read aloud an unusual occupation or experience associated with the "central contestant." During the panel's questioning, the two impostors were allowed to lie while the "central contestant" simply told the truth.

To Tell the Truth reminds me of random people you might meet on the street or people you may know. Their true identity is slowly revealed, and maybe it's because unlike game shows, they don't know who they truly are. There is danger in not knowing and understanding who you are. Uncertainty and confusion about either of these is called an identity crisis. An identity crisis occurs when a person's sense of self becomes insecure and unstable. Most commonly, it occurs when there are major changes in your life.

YOUR IDENTITY IS THROUGH CHRIST

I am a firm believer that you should know as much of your history as possible. Believe it or not, you can erase all doubts regarding your identity when you have knowledge of where you come from. Having discussions with older family members can help you and future generations migrate through life's journey. As a believer, you would want to know how things look from the Bible's perspective, but your true identity is in the Lord Jesus Christ, not in the crisis.

When people have experienced trauma, abuse, rejection, or violation, they store this pain and heartache that they probably will claim as part of their identity. Bad things sometimes happen to good people; but, it does not mean they will end up being total disasters. Your personal growth and development, patience, and character are birthed through hardships.

If you were ever told that you would not be successful or if you were ever told that you would not amount to anything, hopefully, now you know, those words were spoken over you to keep you from trying. Most importantly, whatever unpleasant things happened or whatever unfavorable thing is going on right now, remember those things do not define you. Only Father God can define you. He defines his children by His holy Word. What God says about you is a true representation of your identity. Whenever your enemy tells your story, you are always the victim. However, when you tune in to what God has to say about you through His Word, you are victorious. Keep in mind that God contends with those who contend with you.

YOU PROBABLY HAVE SOME JOSEPH IN YOU

In scripture, Joseph is a character to whom you may be able to relate through his experiences. Joseph didn't let rejections and betrayals define him. His true character defined him. Joseph's name in Hebrew means "he will add." God proved it to be so. There was no lack of favor on his life. His earthly father, Jacob, favored him as well as His heavenly Father. Whenever I think about Joseph, the first thing that comes to mind is that he was a dreamer. Even though he was guilty of being confident and maybe a little cocky, it also appeared that he was a little naïve in how he presented his dream to his brothers. Maybe that was just a setup for how his brother's reaction, mistreatment, and betrayal would play out and how it would propel him into his blessed position. What the enemy meant for bad was reversed and manifested into a wonderful ending.

Joseph's story of how he was dismissed and abandoned by his siblings after he shared his dreams is found in Genesis 37. Later in life, Joseph was forgotten by the very people he sowed into, and yes, this time, he was betrayed by his boss's wife. Even in the crises of life, Joseph's identity was not in his dream or his family.

His identity was not even in his trials. Joseph's identity remained in God.

What I love the most about this story is how before Joseph's birth, God declared a blessing over him through his great-grandfather, Abraham. I love the same thing about my story. God declared Abraham's descendants when He said, "I will give you many descendants. New nations will be born from you, and kings will come from you!" (Genesis 17:6).

Perhaps you are wondering what you have in common with Joseph. Joseph went through several obstacles. Maybe you have as well. Guess what didn't change about Joseph and guess what won't change about you? The crisis he conquered couldn't strip him of his God-given identity, and your crisis will not strip you of who God says you are — His child. Joseph was extremely fruitful and favored. It is important to allow Joseph's story to uplift you to the point of being highly encouraged. You are defined by no other person than the Lord Jesus Christ.

The blessings of the Lord manifested in Joseph's life through all of his trials. He became the ruler of Egypt, an amazing leader. Believe your true identity is in Christ, and God's blessings will manifest in your life as well.

JESUS POPS THE BIG QUESTION

Jesus asked his followers in Matthew 16:15-17, "What are people saying about me, who do they say that I am?" He wasn't asking this question because he lacked identity. He was fully aware of what His disciples were thinking, and He knew who He was. The question was not inspired by self-conceit or egotism. His question was focused on rousing action on the disciples' part. Jesus wanted them to consider their level of faith. The immediate results of His question clearly showed why He even asked.

One of Jesus' followers, Peter, spoke up and boldly confessed, "You're the Christ, the son of the Living God." This test proved the disciple's most authentic level of their faith. Jesus spoke a blessing on Peter and informed him that his answer was not a manifestation of flesh and blood, but it was God working. Keep in mind, God is always at work, moving by His Spirit. He provides revelations of things no one else can reveal.

DISPLAYING THE LOVE OF CHRIST

In July 2002, my family and I moved to Virginia from Supreme Headquarters Allied Powers Europe (SHAPE) Belgium. Although it appeared to be a military assignment, it was far from it. That December, I began working at Defense Supply Center Richmond (DSCR). One day, I was eating lunch in the break room when a lady came in whom I had never met, and she said, "Hello, it's nice to meet you. I know you are a Christian." She proceeded to tell me that there was something different about me. That was an unexpected moment, but she and I became friends, and we still are friends to this day. We both joke now about our initial meeting because all I was doing was eating my lunch alone in the break room. I had no Bible, no t-shirt, and nothing to identify me. I was just being myself. I later learned that you can possess the fragrance of your Father, which is an immediate identifier.

One of the ways we can identify with God is to love like Him. It makes all the difference in the world. Who do you know who doesn't need love? Love is needed more than anything, and love makes the greatest impact. In 1 John 4:20, the Bible says that when people say, "I love God," but they hate their brothers or sisters, they are liars. People who do not love their brothers and sisters, whom they have seen, cannot love God, whom they have never seen.

Get accustomed to loving genuinely and encouraging others. It is up to you to make certain your life reflects your devotion to your heavenly Father. God is love and full of compassion. If you are an imitator of God, that is your desire as well. The Bible does not provide an option to love. Jesus said in John 15:12, "This is my commandment: Love each other in the same way I have loved you."

I will never forget when I was a young adult, and I first read Romans 5:8. I heard it explained in church that God loved me while I was still in sin; he didn't wait for me to become lovable and without sin. That was the answer. I can love the unlovely. How can I not?

Others need to see the love of God in you. How can you love the unlovable? It's easy to love people who are friendly and love you back. Maybe some people have crossed your path who you didn't think deserved your love. We are empowered to love without limits.

It is a true asset to have a solid sense of self. Self-confidence and self-esteem are important to your well-being, physically, mentally, emotionally, as well as spiritually. When you are uncertain of your identity in Christ, it makes it even more difficult to know your purpose.

Make a mental note, God always makes us triumphant in Christ Jesus. Your identity is not in the crisis you endured; it's in the Lord Jesus Christ. Embrace your identity. The Bible says that if you are ashamed of Him, He will be ashamed of you. True believers around the world can attest that there's no shame in our love game. We love hard.

S E V E N

When I Get Where I Am Going, Where Will I Be?

"Man plans, and God laughs."
—*Yiddish expression.*

W hen I was a teenager, a Baptist Training Union session at my church challenged me with this destiny question. "When you get to where you are going, where will you be?" The question infused my mind. As a teenager, this subject raised my curiosity to the point where I began to wonder whether I was spending my time and efforts on the right things. I couldn't help wondering where in the world my contributions would have an impact.

I had questions that I wanted answered. What would my husband be like? If we had children, how many would we have? In what part of the world would we reside, and what kind of careers would we have? My friends had the same questions. Instead of having the "time will tell" kind of attitude, I dreamed, prayed, and visualized the possibilities for my future. I felt strongly that my future would be bright. I knew that I had a key part to play in my destiny.

DREAMS REALIZED

I am reminded of Randy's dream to study psychology at an Iowa college after high school. He and his best friend from kindergarten shared this possibility. Reality set in when my husband knew that enrolling in the college of his dreams was not an option after high school. He was concerned about imposing a financial strain on his parents, so he began researching other options right away.

Like me, Randy is a middle child. We both share an independence that we didn't realize would persist throughout our teen years and manifest throughout our adult lives. It's not that we didn't want or need external assistance from others. Rather, it was that we were willing to take risks and get out in the world to see what would happen. That's what made us even more compatible. Both of us realized that chasing our dreams was worth it, and we would develop our courage, as well as a testimony that would inspire others.

We knew to keep God first. It was echoed throughout our yearbook autographs, graduation cards, and our faith-filled parents' most recommended advice. Thinking of the steps we would have to take in order to fulfill our dreams fueled us with excitement and hope. Now, I realize that in life, you become all the experiences you have encountered. That includes life's highs and lows while journeying from youth to adulthood. At the tender age of seventeen, Randy and I left the nest, not really realizing that God was working out all the good and bad that transpired in our lives for our good. We learned the meaning of Ephesians 1:11, that our destiny was given to us before we were born. This passage confirmed that long before my father met my mother, God had my destiny in mind. It is important to note that God always accomplishes every plan and purpose that He has in mind for you.

As our youngest son, Reagan, was applying to colleges, he applied to a couple of Virginia colleges and a couple of Ohio colleges. Our family took advantage of a visit to James Madison University in Harrisonburg, Virginia, where Reagan seemed to fit in well. When

Reagan received his letter from James Madison regarding his application, he found out he had been waitlisted, which left us disappointed. We knew, however, that the Lord was up to something great. He was accepted to both Ohio colleges, and he decided to attend Miami of Ohio. Even though my husband and I didn't know much about the university, we were pleased. Reagan did three years there, and his senior year, he did a football internship at James Madison University, believe it or not. Reagan attended Pennsylvania State virtually all of his senior year.

As we look back now, we can see that James Madison played an important part of his destiny. His first job was there. In his first year there, he was part of the 2017 Division 1 Football Championship. It gets better. Reagan met his bride, Jessica, there. Jessica is a graduate of James Madison University. Were we upset with the Lord? No way! It is God's way that we cannot see, but it leads us to trust Him always.

Trusting God doesn't mean sitting around twiddling your thumbs. You have to put in the work constantly. If it's a job you want, you have to apply, and if it is a degree you want, you have to position yourself in the area where you will succeed. Blessings are gifts from

Father God that bring joy to our lives. When God blesses with His favor, He empowers us to fulfill His plan for our lives.

Life is often described as a journey. What if it doesn't look like what you imagined? What is this life journey all about anyway? It is about growing, adapting, and making adjustments along the way. In this ever-changing world, life cannot and should not be measured in terms of perfection, but it's the difference you make by being your authentic self and helping others. Your spiritual purpose statement should include that the purpose of living your life is to bring glory to your Lord and Savior, Jesus Christ. Otherwise, what's the point?

Throughout the years, I have given it a lot of thought, and I do a self-evaluation periodically, especially at the end of each year. I ask myself, "Did I make the impact I expected?" If so, should I repeat the strategy? If not, what happened in my life to prevent it? I am always striving to be better.

Both my husband and his best friend were able to get their college degrees. You cannot afford to lock yourself into a "one-size-fits-all" equation. That is the reason we have different testimonies. God will not show up for you necessarily in the same way He showed up for me. One thing you can depend on is that God will show up.

As an individual who prides herself on enjoying the direction in which my life is headed, I absolutely embrace living. Recently, I learned how to pause and be present. We can get so wrapped up in the future that we do not take enough time to embrace the present. I encourage you to bless your own journey as you go. Ask yourself the question I posed at the beginning of this chapter. "When I get where I am going, where will I be?"

I greet each day as priceless and precious because I realize I have been afforded an opportunity to do something that many do not have. Each day brings me closer to my goal. I wake up, look up, get up, pray up, and keep my spirit up. It is because of this that I understand what the psalmist declares in Psalm 118:24, "This is the day that the Lord has made. Let us rejoice and be glad today!"

YOU ARE IN FATHER GOD'S HANDS AND IN HIS PLAN

Do you realize that your life, goals, dreams, and purpose are in God's hands? You are a recipient of God's love, blessings, favor, and grace. I often reflect on the many Biblical characters who set out on epic journeys with a God mission. I think of Moses, who led God's people out of slavery. Joshua led the Israelites across the Jordan River to take possession of the promised land. Abraham found a new nation in an undesignated land that we later learn was Canaan. As one of the rare Biblical female military leaders, Deborah became a singular Biblical figure. She recruited General Barak to stand by her side and tell him God wanted the army of Israel to attack the Canaanites who were persecuting the highland tribes. Jesus was sent into the world to save us from sin by His life, death, and resurrection. He came so we might have a relationship with Father God. You, my friend, have a mission as well. No matter how insignificant you think it is, you're not on Earth by happenstance. You are here to fulfill the role of an optimist. The Lord will place people on your path who need that type of energy. No matter what comes to hinder you, by all means, fulfill the role and complete the mission.

Jeremiah 29:11 keeps me motivated on my journey. The Lord says, "I say this because I know what I am planning for you. I have good plans for you, not plans to hurt you. I will give you hope and a good future." I am sold out to the idea that my goal is to make someone's life better. I hope when I get to where I am destined, my life will be regarded as well worth the journey, and my testimony will be that I did my best to help bring someone's destiny into fruition.

Start acting like your future self. Believe me, when you change your perspective, it builds the kind of character that will make you appreciative of the Lord at work in your life.

Below, I offer a three-fold formula that will help fill your life with joy, help you enjoy each day, and bless your journey.

✓ Initiate a special time for daily prayer and a meditation schedule.
One of the best ways I know to start my day is with prayer. The benefits of a prayer life outweigh the worries and the cares of life. It has been said that prayer reduces feelings of isolation, anxiety, and fear as well. Praying to Father God is as easy as talking to your best friend, especially if He is your best friend. It's all in the relationship. If that's your area that you need to build, I suggest you start right where you are. Talk to Him daily. Read and meditate on His

promises throughout His Word. Use times of meditation to provide you with calmness, peace, and balance. As a result, meditation can benefit you spiritually and emotionally, and it can improve your overall health.

✓ Realize and accept that your life will not be perfect, and neither will you.

Sometimes, what you had planned will not happen, and sometimes, things will happen you did not plan. According to Deuteronomy 31:8, "the Lord Himself will go before you. He will be with you; He will not leave you or forget you. Don't be afraid and don't worry."

✓ Take ownership of your vision.

It is a known fact that successful people have vision. A clear vision of your life enhances your life. How can you know when you have reached your desired outcome? We learn from Proverbs 29:18 that those who obey what they have been taught are happy, but those who hear no word from God are uncontrolled. My pastor says this all the time. "Teaching sticks to you like grits."

Learn what God says about your life in His Word and fulfill God's plan. Dare to seek God's will and dive off the board in faith to receive His wonderful destiny for your life.

E I G H T

Bring Your Flavor To The Table

"Your smile is your logo. Your personality is your business card. How you leave others feeling after having an experience with you becomes your trademark."

— *Jay Danzie*

I'm often asked, "What is one thing you know now that you wish you'd known in your youth?" I wish I had known that not being like everyone else in my circle was okay. In fact, it was more than okay; it was perfect. I wish I had known that trying to fit in was not necessary. I wish I had known that using what the Lord gave me to inspire someone else is better than trying to be like someone else.

OPERATING IN MY GIFT

I remember when I received my calling to preach the gospel. It was emotional and exciting. I had not prayed to serve as a minister. While growing up in church, I loved singing in junior choir, helping with Vacation Bible School, being the secretary of Sunday School, and the president of the Youth Club. I began public speaking at a very young age. My teenage years were a time when I was just myself, and I felt good being me. I was excited that people wanted to hear what I had to say. The fact that there were so many women preachers by the time I was a young adult perhaps made me notice it because this was now my spiritual lane.

The opportunity to see these women operate in their gifts was amazing. I admired several of them and even considered making my presentations similar to those that I either saw on television or video tapes or heard on cassette tapes. I quickly realized that it was easier to be me. It was already nerve-racking to be asked to speak, (even though I was not new to it), so why should I devote time or energy trying to be like someone else? If that was even necessary, they would have called on Evangelist Someone Else. I needed to not only be me, but also I needed to be comfortable being me. I came to the conclusion that I had to respect the anointing on my life. I also found that there is nothing wrong with admiring how God uses others, but I learned how to appreciate my flow. My teaching and preaching gifts come from God. The least I could do was to work with God, accept my gifts, talents, and abilities, and allow Him to use me as He chooses.

BE THE CHANGE YOU WANT TO SEE

Good news: We are called to bring flavor to the blandness. We are called to make a difference. Salt is used for a variety of purposes. Before refrigeration, salt was used commonly to preserve food. For the sake of this discussion, salt is symbolic of realizing you can make a difference in the universe.

There are a number of references to salt in the Bible. The first one that comes to mind is an amazing eye-opener on the subject of making a difference. It is found in Matthew 5:13. This passage informs you that you are flavorful. "You are the salt of the earth. But if the salt loses its salty taste, it cannot be made salty again. It is good for nothing, except to be thrown out and walked on."

My mom has been fortunate to visit us everywhere we have been stationed. On one of her Maryland trips, she always would ask us to pass her the salt at dinner time. I was so afraid that she would develop hypertension, not just from her visits, but from what she consumed at home. As a result of my fear, I offered her other substitutes, but for her, there was nothing like the real thing. She never liked bland food, but that's common for most folk. However, have you ever thought about what would happen if we added salt to the food, and it still had no flavor? Jesus is informing us not to worry about making something salty again, but He wants us to display what I like to refer to as saltiness maintained. Hold what you got. Let's face it, the world can be a cold dark place, but you are more than capable of making a difference. One of the most powerful lessons I have learned in life is to let go of what culture dictates is right and embrace, display, and stand on what the gospel truth says. Do not allow yourself to become bland and flavorless.

As one of my favorite chefs told me, salt's main use in cooking is to suppress other flavors like bitterness and to balance sweetness. I responded, "That's it!" Believers are called to suppress bitterness, toxic, and anything ungodly and balance the sweetness, leaving their own unique flavor. Just as salt gives flavor to food, believers and Christ's followers add flavor to the world by living out the lives He has called us to live. According to Romans 12:2, we are not conformers; we are transformers.

On one of our military assignments, which we refer to as missions, we spent time at Fort Jackson in South Carolina. One of the first things on our list was finding a church home that God purposed for us. God sent us to Rehoboth Baptist. We didn't realize it at the time, but we were sent to be salt. The pastor of that season of our lives was Dr. George G. Gaymon. There was no doubt that he was a progressive leader sent to change the community. We were young in age, young in ministry, energetic, and extremely excited. We represented something new that we now believe our pastor had been looking forward to in his ministry. Serving under his pastorate was life-changing for us.

Pastor Gaymon pushed, protected, encouraged, and corrected us. Through challenges, he made sure we did not lose our saltiness. To be useful to God's plan, we had to humble ourselves, making all the spiritual gifts and teachings we brought with us subservient to the leadership of the house. We became salt in God's hand. Like every other assignment, we were there to support the pastor's vision for a season of time. We watched the transition from traditionalism to mainstream progressivism unfold in front of our eyes. As a result, a number of military families, many of whom brought saltiness to the ministry, followed.

YOUR FLAVOR MATTERS

I am elated that one of my life lessons learned is to never try to fit in. Authentic people will respect you and what you have to offer if you bring your unique flavor to the table. I cannot emphasize enough that comparing yourself to others is never helpful. When it happens, speak to yourself and remind yourself that it is fine to bring your personality into any room in which you find yourself. It is like putting a puzzle together. What happens if you place one piece in a space where it does not belong? Do you force it? I do not recommend that. Likewise, everyone you meet on your path will not think like you. They won't have the same gifts and talents as you either. However, if you can leverage your uniqueness, which sets you apart from everyone else and creates a sustainable competitive advantage, you will find that everyone wins.

I was told recently that my smile is appreciated in the workplace as a greeting in meetings, conferences, and other presentations. My smile and personality draw people to me. Our church has a catchphrase, and we emphasize it every week, "Your smile is your favor." Since I am a student in this life, and because our church is a teaching ministry, I live by the principles that I am taught. There is no need to reinvent the wheel. When you receive spiritual principles, just follow the instructions and reap the blessings.

Know that each step you take is pre-ordained by God. That alone makes the journey worthwhile. You can walk in faith, encourage others, and be fearless when some of the puzzle pieces don't fit. Remember to use your gifts, talents, and abilities to keep the Earth seasoned. Your saltiness matters. How can you salty up the Earth? You can spread the message of God's love and His redemption story. Luke 14:35 says that salt that is flavorless has become ineffective; it cannot be used for the soil or for manure; it is thrown away. In order to be effective in the kingdom of God, your foundation must be aligned to God's Word. "Let those with ears use them and listen."

If everyone followed this approach to life, there would be nothing missing. All the gifts would be flowing, operating, and making the difference. Step up to the plate, knowing you're the right one, and you bring the right flavor to complete the mission. Life is not hit or miss. If your destiny includes greatness, know that the world is counting on you and the flavor you add to your environment. When you are your authentic self, ultimately, it makes God one proud Dad.

•

GWENDOLYN CODY-DAVIS

N I N E

Slay Your Race

"I have observed something else under the sun. The fastest runner doesn't always win the race, and the strongest warrior doesn't always win the battle. The wise sometimes go hungry, and the skillful are not necessarily wealthy. Those who are educated don't always lead successful lives. It is all decided by chance by being in the right place at the right time."

—*Ecclesiastes 9:11*

Whether they admit it or not, everyone you meet is running a race. It appears that everyone is busy, running the race of life. Some days, you may feel victorious, and some days you may feel defeated but keep running. Remember to keep your pace — it's your race.

The race of life is such a journey. The unique aspect of it is that your lane will not look like the person in the lane next to you, but your lane is unique to you. There is power in learning to control what takes place in your own lane. You will not be able to own your lane until you shake off anything, and everything that is extra weight.

While the race is not won by the swiftest, runners cannot get far if they are weighed down with the cares of life. From Hebrews 12:1, we are reminded that we are surrounded by a great cloud of people whose lives are examples of what faith means. Let's run the race that is before us and never give up. It's important for us to remove anything that would get in the way, and eliminate the sin that so easily holds us back.

It may not be easy to remove everything from your life that would get in the way. Yes, people and situations sometimes will get in the way. No matter what kind of race you're running, literally, figuratively, or spiritually, realize that a race has excitement and hype associated with it as well.

HEALTHY COMPETITION

During my senior year of high school, I participated in the "Miss Black Awareness Contest." This pageant, which was actually a fundraiser, was held during Black History Month in 1978 at our local Young Men's Christian Association (YMCA). There were twelve participants, and we competed in several categories including talent and modeling. I wanted to excel in all categories. Competing was about having fun and inspiring younger girls to engage in these types of activities to help them gain self-confidence. As a talent for this competition, I played the theme song from the popular 1970s soap opera, The Young and the Restless. I invested hours practicing at home as well as with my piano teacher, Ms. Juanita Varner, who also was our wedding pianist. I will always remember her for being so patient and encouraging. She just knew I could do it.

I was nervous when I took my seat at the piano. I just kept remembering all the things I learned about the piece, and how pleased I wanted the audience to be, especially the judges.

I was happy to be announced the winner. Months later, the winner and the two-runner ups were invited to be a part of the Annual Rose Parade. I had marched in the band, playing clarinet in the Rose Parade since junior high; however, this opportunity was much different. We were riding in a convertible owned by my mom's boss. My dad was our driver. I will never forget the feeling of pride that we had that day. I believe these kinds of occasions helped to shape and inspire me to work hard, and they inspired others to do the same. The bonding was great as well. It was this event that helped me realize I possessed a "competitive spirit."

The race of life is like a contest. It is an event for sure. Remind yourself that it's not how fast you run your race that matters. What matters is your steady momentum and your determination to complete the race. Determination is half the battle. You have to practice, position yourself, and take pride in every single detail of the task at hand. Do all the things you can to stay motivated to complete every project and task you have undertaken. Perhaps you have heard it said that life is a marathon, not a sprint. Simply put, a marathon takes a great deal of time to complete, while a sprint doesn't take long at all.

In August 2022, I had the honor of participation in my first Annual Independent Black Author Expo in Hyattsville, Maryland. I invited old and new friends to attend, and many came out to support me. I had the opportunity to speak for the first time as an author in public on my why. On that day, I will never forget that one of my girlfriends for over thirty-five years told me that her big brother Randy and I set a high bar for our family and friends, and she told me how proud she is of me. That resonated with me for weeks because sometimes you feel like you're not making a difference, or you feel that no one even notices what you have done. I was delighted to be reminded that I'm in my lane, fulfilling my mission.

According to the law of gravity, whatever goes up must come down. My highest goal in life is to inspire and to encourage others. Did I really think that I would not receive encouragement in return? Thank God it does return just when it's needed the most.

TIME MANAGEMENT

My husband often reflects on his military career, and I never tire of hearing his stories. Both of us will be engrafted forever with the lessons learned. Recently, we were discussing physical training during his military service. PT is what soldiers call it. Every year, the United States Army evaluates each soldier's physical and mental abilities through a fitness test. Among the events in the testing program is a two-mile run. In this mobility event, the soldier's aerobic endurance is tested. He/she is awarded points based on a grading scale. The grading scale, for example, informs you, based on your age, that sixty points is the minimum score. Mentally, you know that the sixty points is the minimum score based on your time. In most cases, the run is conducted on a track, which means you will not be the only one on the track that day taking the test. There's no doubt about it. It is you against the clock, and in order to succeed, you must slay.

In order to complete the two miles, you cannot have any physical assistance from anyone. You cannot stop, and you are not allowed breaks. You must complete the entire two miles. The requirement plays on your mind. Imagine the soldier standing at the starting line. His/her mind is focused on the standard and the clock. To overcome the mental and physical ability of it all, you have to practice well in advance for the test. That is one of the strategies. For example, it makes no sense to go out and consume an eighteen-ounce steak or a keg of beer the night before the exam. If you do, it is highly unlikely you will pass this type of event. The good thing is that there is someone whose job it is to provide your time and pace at the quarter and half mile points during the test. This lets you know if you should speed up because you are behind, or you know that you can coast your way in because you are ahead. When you get to the halfway point, you begin to get a sense of yourself. The adrenaline usually speeds up. You get a rush. You see the finish line, and you know you are definitely in execution mode. Your self-worth, value, and appreciation for all your efforts are finally realized and respected. By now, your faith and confidence have reached a new level.

Whenever you strive to become the best version of yourself, you will go out of your way to shape your body and mind to perform at a high level. You develop and execute a plan.

Those who fail the PT test must retest. Even if you experience such a setback, you cannot give up. There is always a way to reach your desired goal. Sometimes, it may involve humbling yourself, seeking assistance, and taking your work more seriously.

My husband shared a presentation recently, which we refer to as a positive snack, on one of my social media platforms about clock management. His emphasis was, "You can still get it done, as long as there is time on the clock." He referenced an Old Testament story found in 2 Kings 4:8-37. In the story, the prophet, Elisha, goes to Shunem where an important woman lived. She begged Elisha to stay and eat. Every time Elisha passed by, he stopped there to eat. The woman said to her husband, "I know that this is a holy man of God who passes by our house all the time. Let's make a small room on the roof and put a bed in the room for him. We can put a table, a chair, and a lamp stand there. Then, when he comes by, he can stay there."

Well, guess what? One day Elisha came to the woman's house, and the room was ready for him. He went to his room and rested. He said to his servant, Gehazi, "Call the Shunammite woman." When the servant had called her, she stood in front of him. Elisha then told his servant, "Now say to her, you have gone to all this trouble for us. What can I do for you? Do you want me to speak to the king or the commander of the army for you?" She answered, "I live among my own people."

Elisha said to Gehazi, "But what can we do for her?" He answered, "She has no son, and her husband is old." Then, Elisha said to Gehazi, "Call her." When he called her, she stood in the doorway. Then, Elisha said, "About this time next year, you will hold a son in your arms." The woman said, "No, master, man of God, don't lie to me, your servant!" However, the woman became pregnant and gave birth to a son at that time the next year just as Elisha had told her. The boy grew up, and one day, he went out to his father who was with the grain harvesters. The boy said to his father, "My head! My head!"

The father said to his servant, "Take him to his mother!" The servant took him to his mother, and he laid on his mother's lap until noon. Then, he died. She took him up and laid him on Elisha's bed, shut the door, and left. She called to her husband, "Send me one of the servants and one of the donkeys. Then, I can go quickly to the man of God and return." The husband said, "Why do you want to go to him today? It isn't the New Moon or the Sabbath day." She said, "It will be alright."

Then, she saddled the donkey and said to her servant, "Lead on. Don't slow down for me unless I tell you." She went to Elisha at Mount Carmel. When he saw her coming from far away, he said to his servant, Gehazi, "Look, there's the Shunammite woman. Run to meet her and ask, 'Are you alright? Is your husband alright? Is the boy alright?'" Gehazi did, and she answered, "Everything is alright." Then, she came to Elisha at the hill and grabbed his feet. Gehazi came near to pull her away, but Elisha said to him, "Leave her alone. She's very upset, and the LORD has not told me about it. He has hidden it from me."

She said, "Master, did I ask you for a son? Didn't I tell you not to lie to me?"

Elisha said to Gehazi, "Get ready. Take my walking stick in your hand and go quickly. If you meet anyone, don't say hello. If anyone greets you, don't respond. Lay my walking stick on the boy's face." The boy's mother said, "As surely as the LORD lives and as you live, I won't leave you!" Elisha got up and followed her.

Gehazi went on ahead and laid the walking stick on the boy's face, but the boy did not talk or move. Then, Gehazi went back to meet Elisha. "The boy has not awakened," he said.

When Elisha came into the house, the boy was lying dead on his bed. Elisha entered the room and shut the door. Only he and the boy were in the room. Elisha prayed to the LORD, went to the bed, and lay on the boy, putting his mouth on the boy's mouth, his eyes on the boy's eyes, and his hands on the boy's hands. He stretched himself out on top of the boy. Soon, the boy's skin became warm. Elisha turned away and walked around the room. Then, he went back and put himself on the boy again. The boy sneezed seven times and opened his eyes. Elisha called Gehazi and said, "Call the Shunammite!" When she came, Elisha said, "Pick up your son." She came in and fell at Elisha's feet, bowing her face down to the floor. Then, she picked up her son and went out.

What I like about this story is that it not only is a wonderful example of Christ-like character traits that we should all desire, but it also provides an example of a brilliant strategy for how to leverage what you have (faith) to get what you need (a miracle). Over the years, this story has become one of my favorites. Interestingly enough, we do not know this woman's name. She is known by the name of her town, Shunem. The Bible refers to her as the Shunammite Woman. However, there are so many adjectives that delightfully describe this woman. She was generous, hospitable, and enterprising. One of the first things you may think of when hearing about this Shunammite woman is how she offered a room in her home to the prophet Elisha. One of her priorities was that she made a connection with the man of God, and that connection registered in heaven.

My husband's presentation went a little like this. In gridiron football, clock management is a game of strategy that focuses on two clocks — the game clock and the play clock — to achieve a desired result. Clock management is a very important facet of the game. The goal is to manipulate the time on the clock to reach a desired outcome. However, life plays the defense. Life issues come to cause you to suffer a loss when you could have experienced a win. Keep in mind, the goal is to apply the strategy to manipulate the clock to your advantage.

The most essential lesson in running the race of life is to know that it's your own race. Own your race. Realize from the onset that you can only control the things that you can control. Your time and energy are two of your most precious resources. Use them both on self-improvement while setting your pace on your race. Just like an active-duty soldier, you allow no one or nothing to derail your goals when you focus on your lane. Time is a valuable asset. It is essential to note that time is a nonrenewable resource that can never be recycled.

THERE IS ONLY ONE PRIZE

The Bible tells us in 1 Corinthians 9:24-25 that all runners in the race run, but only one gets the prize. This passage encourages us to run in such a way to get the prize. Everyone who competes in the games goes into strict training. They do not only get a crown, but they get a crown that will last forever.

The race of life is not always easy to run. Some days, you don't feel like running, and some days, you don't feel like keeping pace. Sometimes, I reflect on the old saying, "If it's not one thing, it's another." Through it all, run on. Your reward is greater than your trial.

I cannot reiterate enough how important it is to never focus on how fast you run your race. It's not about how to rush to finish the race. The true beauty of your story lies in savoring each moment, celebrating each victory, and realizing that every loss serves as a lesson to go harder on the next opportunity. At the end, each runner will each give an account to God for how he or she ran the race. You should live for that moment, knowing that the joy of your journey is to not only have a plan, but to execute that plan. Faith is belief in action. As long as there is time remaining on the clock, expect great things to happen.

GWENDOLYN CODY-DAVIS

T E N

Decoding The Myth Of Unforgiveness

*"See to it that no one fails to obtain the grace of God;
that no "root of bitterness" springs up and causes
trouble, and by it, many become defiled."*
—Hebrews 12:15

H ave you ever held on to a grudge so tightly and for so long that you forgot the details of what made you take such a route? Psychologists define forgiveness as a conscious, deliberate decision to release feelings toward a person's behavior. There is an old saying that says, "Forgiveness never excuses the wrongs against us or waters down the awful nature of an offense." However, forgiveness is a gift that frees you to live. Unforgiveness, on the hand, is when you are reluctant to forgive someone for deceiving or breaking your trust.

Let's dispel the myth of unforgiveness. You need to know that forgiveness does not necessarily mean that the person is someone with whom you should hang out or have lunch. It's a myth that forgiveness makes you the offender's best friend. That's not true. I remember my mother saying, "I'm going to feed that person with a long-handled spoon." That simply means I forgive and respect them, but I'm not going to get too close to them because they have hurt me once. While you use the golden rule by treating them how you would like to be treated, you also must try hard not to put yourself in a position to be hurt again.

True forgiveness empowers the forgiver to recognize the pain suffered without allowing the pain to define them. This brings a sense of freedom that not only allows you to keep moving forward on your life's journey and heal, but also it allows you to help someone along the way who gets stuck in the poison of unforgiveness. There is no amount of money that you could possibly earn that comes close to having a peace of mind. Inability to forgive prevents you from appreciating pure calmness and peace in your mind and your spirit, which causes you not to progress in life as you should.

LET IT GO

You will never experience inner peace until you forgive all those who you feel have wronged you. If you truly forgive, you are doing the work necessary to not only be free, but also to be used by God. There are many people who want and need to know how you did it. Mark 11:25-26 informs you that during your prayer time, if you are angry with someone, you should forgive them, so your heavenly Father also will forgive you. It makes perfect sense. We serve a loving and forgiving God. Maybe you will meet someone on your Christian journey who, like you, desires to be an imitator of the Lord Jesus. What a great witness to the power of God when forgiveness becomes a part of your testimony.

Forgiving someone does not make you weak. Forgiving others also does not mean you are dismissing or even encouraging their wrong behavior. Forgiveness means admitting the wrong that you feel has been done to you but not allowing yourself to hold onto a grudge that has not been assigned to you. You have two choices when it comes to forgiveness. Will you forgive your offenders or not? If you decide, "Yes, I will do forgive them," then know that you will reap the benefits of being one who forgives. If you decide you will not forgive those who have wronged you, the Bible says in Matthew 18:34 that you will end up imprisoned. Jesus is speaking to Christians who refuse to forgive, who hold grudges and harbor bitter feelings. These people will be turned over to torturous thoughts, feelings of misery, and agonizing unrest within. If you are tormented, how can you win and see your dreams come to pass?

Matthew 18:34 also tells the story of how a king began to collect money owed to him by a servant. The servant owed several million dollars. The servant did not have enough money to pay his master, the king. The master ordered that everything the servant owned, including his wife and children, should be sold to repay the debt. The servant fell on his knees and begged the king to be patient with him, and that he would repay everything he owed. The master felt sorry for his servant and told him he did not have to pay back his debt. Then, he let the servant go free.

Later, the same servant found another servant who owed him a few dollars. He grabbed him around the neck and said, "Pay me the money you owe me!" The other servant fell on his knees and begged him to be patient with him. He told him that he would repay all that he owed. The master heard about this and was angered. He called his servant in. "You evil servant! Because you begged me to forget what you owed, I told you that you did not have to pay anything. You should have shown mercy to that other servant just as I showed mercy to you." The master put the servant in prison to be punished until he could pay everything he owed. This king did what our heavenly Father will do if we do not forgive our brothers or sisters from our hearts.

In Matthew 6:15 we are encouraged that yes, if we forgive others for their sins, our Father in heaven also will forgive us for our sins. However, if we don't forgive others, our Father will not forgive us.

Forgiveness is a process. It is safe to say that this process is highly unique and personal to every individual. I encourage you to make a serious decision about establishing boundaries and reevaluating your relationships. Establishing boundaries can be a game changer and can help you find the peace you need in your forgiveness process.

James challenges us in James 2:14. He says, "My brothers and sisters, if people say they have faith, but do nothing, their faith is worth nothing. Can faith like that save them?"

Have you ever been lied to by someone at your job who claimed to be in the know about a job selection or a promotion? A close friend shared with me about a dream he almost achieved. He emphasized the fact that it takes the power of the Holy Spirit to forgive.

Imagine the "misinformed" with advanced knowledge leaks the news directly to you or through someone you know and trust. You welcome that news and the messenger because it is exactly what your little itching ears want to hear. You rationalize and entertain the news saying, "This is great news; it must be from God! Wonderful! God is good!" The trouble comes when management releases the official notice, and your name is not on the list. Instantly, you feel rejection and despair. You feel like a fool because you bought into the lie the liar so expertly sold. How do you deal with this now? It's never too late to forgive.

Forgiveness is one of the major attributes of having a personal relationship with Christ. 1 John 1:9 lets us know that if we confess our sins, God will forgive our sins because we can trust Him to do what is right. He will cleanse us from all the wrongs we have done. Our God is faithful, forgiving, and loving.

On our second military assignment at SHAPE Belgium, we lived on the economy, so we were able to gain a greater appreciation of the local culture. We lived on the economy during our first tour as well, so we were excited about being a part of the community. We found what appeared to be the perfect house for our family. We spent the weekend in Germany and arrived back home in Ghlin on a Sunday night to find our house had been broken into. That was the first time this had happened to us, and we felt how all victims must feel — violated and helpless. Living in Europe at that time was quite different from living in the states. Calling the police and contacting our insurance company was different. Even so, we pressed on, trying to keep our young sons calm and secure. Neither of us had forgiveness on our minds initially. How could this have happened? First, it was difficult to tell what had been stolen because the thought that someone had been in our house uninvited stung like a bee. How do you recover quickly?

Along with feeling violated, we felt unsecured. We didn't have ADT security services or any form of protection against something like this from reoccurring. We finally received the peace we needed to continue the journey after we released forgiveness to whomever violated our personal property. Unforgiveness has a root cause that you need to understand fully. Bitterness is at the root of unforgiveness, which is toxic. Scientifically, a toxin is often considered a specific type of poison; thus, unforgiveness is considered a poisonous prison.

At this point in my life, forgiving is just easier. I feel lighter, and less stressed when I forgive as quickly as possible. My daily prayer is that the Lord help me cast any wrong directed at me into the sea of forgiveness. Forgiveness does not mean you forget the offense. But, don't give up on God. Whenever the pain of unforgiveness comes up, refrain from rehearsing it in your mind. Each time you do, you get further away from forgiveness.

Forgiving someone who you feel has wronged you is one of the most powerful things you can do for yourself, not to mention, your offender. Father God sees you. Father God loves you. When He sees you following His examples, your reward is not unnoticed or forgotten. Sowing seeds of forgiveness does not mean you allow someone to use you as a doormat.

Keep in mind, you were created in God's image, and you are sons and daughters of the Most High God. How can you be of that caliber and be a doormat? According to Philippians 2:14-15, you should do everything without complaining or arguing. Then, you will be innocent and without any wrong. You will be God's children without fault. However, you are living with crooked and mean people all around you, among whom you shine like stars in the dark world.

Here are seven strategies to decode the myth of unforgiveness, make positive efforts in your life, receive your healing, and finish strong.

✓ Acknowledge the hurt.

If you never acknowledge that you felt the pain caused by someone or something, how can you receive the help you need to overcome it? You can come out of denial and admit your feelings to someone trustworthy and let them know that you are hurting.

✓ Set healthy realistic boundaries.

Setting healthy boundaries is not sinful. When you are able to repay your offender with forgiveness, do not feel as if you have to give this person another chance to hurt you. Maybe they won't. Maybe they have learned their lesson. However, if this is not the case, break the cycle.

✓ Recognize there is power in forgiveness.

When you forgive others, you are not only setting the offender free, but also you are freeing yourself. When you know better, you are better at doing it.

✓ Practicing forgiveness helps you to stay physically and mentally fit.

There is no better heart than a forgiving heart. Some of the perks include: lower levels of depression, anxiety, and hostility, higher self-esteem, and self-confidence, which creates a new zest for life.

✓ Tap into God's peace and stay there.

There is a reminder in Philippians 4:7 urging you to not be anxious about anything but in every situation, by prayer and petition and with thanksgiving, to present your requests to God. The peace of God, which transcends all understanding, will guard your hearts and your minds in Christ Jesus. For me, the key words in verse seven are "peace," "transcends," "guard," and "minds." You owe it to yourself to experience God's peace. The older I become, the more I seem to tap into God's peace. Nothing in the world compares to the peace of God.

✓ Remember, forgiveness is usually not instantaneous. There is no shame in working through pain and loss. When you have faith in God, His words become more real, and you always should trust what is real.

✓ Forgive yourself.

Are there some things from which you need to forgive yourself? Have you ever disappointed yourself and felt it was your own fault? Have you ever failed to measure up to what you expected? If you answered yes to at least one of the questions above, believe there are times in our lives when we wish we could start over. However, instead of spending energy on things we cannot change, I recommend using that energy to erase or begin a new page. You just may have to recycle several times before you get it right. However, the old saying is really true. "If at first, you don't succeed, keep trying." The truth is you will succeed if you don't give up.

GWENDOLYN CODY-DAVIS

Epilogue

Now that you have completed reading this book, you have information and strategies to transform your dreams into your realities. You have the ability and capability to finish strong.

Gone are the days when you are always learning, but you are unable to apply what you have learned to improve the seasons of your life. Now is the time to incorporate this information and lessons learned with your life experiences while operating in your full truth.

The following is a summary of the concepts discussed in this book to help you become a dream executing impactful individual.

ONE: The Power Of Small Beginnings This chapter helps you understand that your starting point is always important. Just because it's the starting point does not mean it's your ending. Be grateful and stay grounded. Your humble beginning is key to your overall success.

TWO: Overcoming Failures Surrounding yourself with successful people is bound to rub off on you. Your failures can help encourage someone. Shut down the negative voices and make up your mind that despite every obstacle you face, you were born to win.

THREE: Keep The Dream Alive In life, you either work on your dreams to bring them to pass, or you just keep on dreaming; the choice is yours. Without a course of action, your dreams remain on layaway. Without a payment (self-motivation and encouragement), you can never pick it up.

FOUR: Next Level Integrity Core values are ingredients that we can never leave out of our lives. They are never inappropriate. Core values should be taught, emphasized, and emulated.

FIVE: Laughter Is Like A Medicine With No Side Effects If not for our joy, how will the world know who we are? One way we express joy is through laughter. It helps reduce bad stress and offers powerful health benefits. Keep smiling, Keep laughing. Keep the joy.

SIX: Identity Crisis — Do Not Allow Anyone Go Define You People and situations do not define you. If you are a child of God, you are defined by your Father God. Everything His Word says about you is true.

SEVEN: When I Get Where I'm Going, Where will I Be? God is always up to something spectacular in our lives. No, He has not forgotten you. While trusting Him, put in the work necessary to bring your dreams into fruition.

EIGHT: Bring Your Flavor To The Table You are the salt, and you are the light. Remember that each step you take is pre-ordained by God. Be yourself while making improvements along the way. Someone needs what only you have to give.

NINE: Slay Your Race Since the race is not won by the swiftest, runners cannot get very far if they are weighed down with the cares of life. Shake off the burdens, the cares, and the worries, and set your pace. I will see you at the finish line.

TEN: Decoding The Myth Of Unforgiveness Keep in mind that forgiveness is a process. Make a command decision on whether boundaries are needed. Find the peace and the calm needed in your forgiveness process. Forgive everyone who you feel has wronged you, including you.

About
The Author

Gwendolyn Cody-Davis, who likes to be called "Cody," is a dynamic servant-leader of the gospel of Jesus Christ. Presently, she serves as a licensed and ordained elder at Blessed Hope Community Church (BHCC) in Prince George, Virginia under the anointed leadership of Bishop C. E. Wiley, Sr., and Pastor Amelia J. Wiley.

She is a native of Thomasville, Georgia and a product of the Thomasville City Schools. While in high school, Cody entered into a romance, which God has since transformed into a 42-year (and counting) marriage with her best friend and husband, Randy M. Davis. Lovingly, she refers to him as her African king!

Cody earned a Master of Business Administration from Averett University in Danville, Virginia.

Cody is a member of Iota Phi Lambda Sorority, Inc., Gamma Delta Chapter located in Richmond Virginia. Cody loves mentoring young ladies in the field of business and encouraging others to fulfill dreams.

As a civil servant, Cody has over 30 years in the federal government. Currently, she is a customer account specialist at the Defense Logistics Agency, at Fort Belvoir, Virginia. Cody currently resides with her husband in Chester, Virginia. They are the owners of NOMOLAC, LLC.

They are also the proud parents of two adult sons: Ryan, their oldest son, and a beautiful daughter-in-love, Kiandra, and Reagan, their youngest son, and another beautiful daughter-in-love, Jessica.

Connect With Me

Email: gwendavisgava@gmail.com

Website: https://gwendolyncody-davis.com

For additional resources on how to finish strong despite setbacks, VIP Warriors are invited to register your book on https://gwendolyncody-davis.com/

FB: Love Letters from the MuM

IG: gwendolyncodydavis

Linkedin: gwendolyncodydavis

Twitter: Gwendolyn Cody-Davis aka "the MuM"

GWENDOLYN CODY-DAVIS

Made in the USA
Middletown, DE
12 June 2023